Richard Davies

IN VOGUE
75 Years of Style

IN VOGUE
75 Years of Style

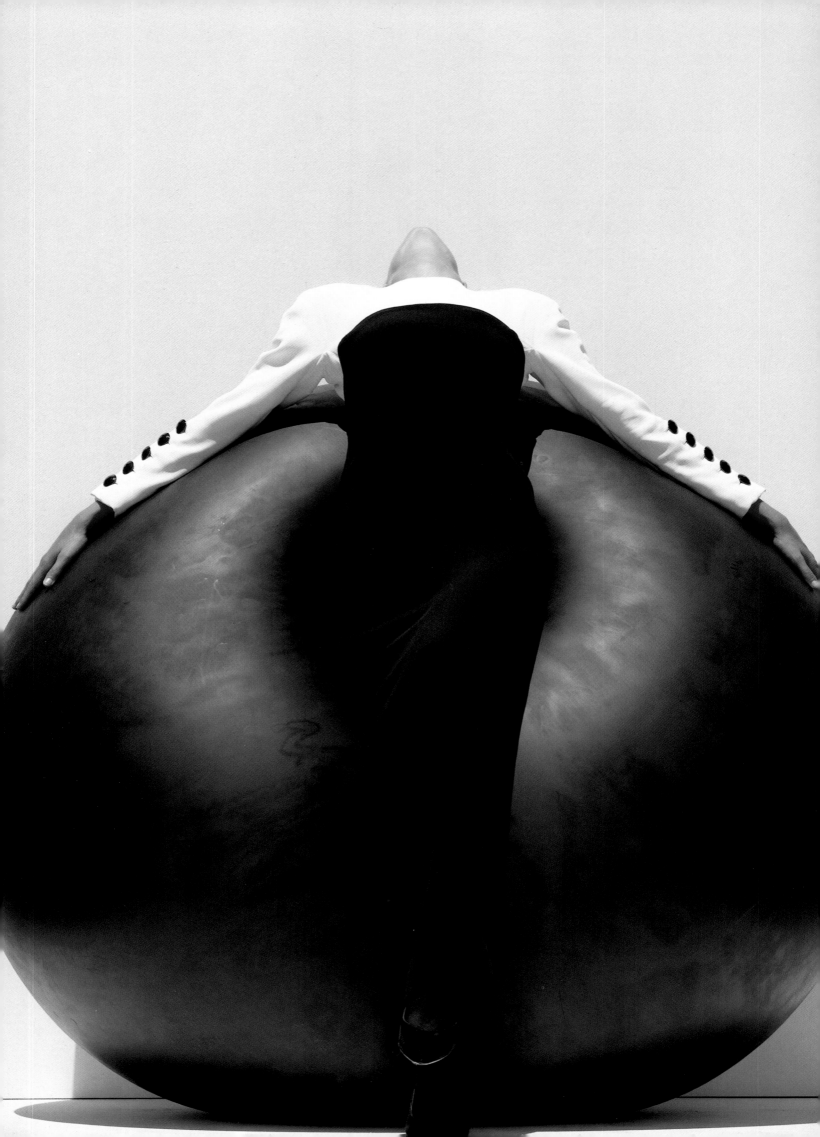

GEORGINA HOWELL

IN VOGUE

75 YEARS OF STYLE

CONDÉ NAST BOOKS

London Sydney Auckland Johannesburg

For Christopher

Text copyright © Georgina Howell 1991

Photographs copyright © copyright owners
see pages 248-249

First published in 1991 as a Condé Nast Book by Random Century Ltd
Random Century House, 20 Vauxhall Bridge Road
London SW1V 2SA

Random Century Australia Pty Ltd
20 Alfred Street, Milsons Point, Sydney, NSW 2061, Australia

Random Century (NZ) Ltd
18 Poland Road, Glenfield
Auckland 10 New Zealand

Century Hutchinson South Africa Pty Ltd
PO Box 337, Bergvlei 2012, South Africa

British Cataloguing in Publication data

Howell, Georgina
In Vogue
I. Title
391

ISBN 0 7126 4791 0

Designed by Paul Bowden Design
Picture research by Robin Muir

Printed and bound in West Germany by Mohndruck

Acknowledgements

It was Alex Kroll, former editor of *Vogue*'s books department, for whom I wrote the first *In Vogue*, and it was his idea, and Philip Norman's, that I should bring it up to date: thanks to them both. Georgina Boosey, *Vogue*'s managing editor, smiled on the project from the start and oiled the wheels along the way.

My special thanks go to Hilary Arnold, publishing director for Century non-fiction and head of Condé Nast books, and to Sophie Figgis, my careful editor there, for undertaking the new *In Vogue*. In their capable hands the book prospered and became a thing of the 1990s. It was a great pleasure to work with them. I am also grateful to Catherine Carpenter for considerable editorial help.

We were lucky indeed that Paul Bowden accepted the invitation to rethink the book visually. No one could have done it better or with more sense of period. Thanks also to Raphael Whittle, his able assistant.

Enormous help came from an unexpected quarter when *Vogue*'s archivist and contributing editor Robin Muir arrived to do the picture research. Thanks to his great visual sense, expertise and total recall of where and when the pictures first appeared, he knocked weeks off the work schedule: 'Bit of a change in the library' said David Bailey - 'someone who knows what's what'.

I would like to thank *Vogue*'s entire gallery of great photographers for the use of their remarkable pictures, and specially David Bailey, Horst and Irving Penn.

Vivien Hamley of Hamiltons Photographers worked tirelessly to track down Norman Parkinson originals and Lydia Cresswell-Jones of the Beaton archive, Sotheby's, London, helped us recapture the past.

I would like to think that the modernized *In Vogue* has matched the transformation of the magazine itself into the crisp, surprising and energetic product of its present editor-in-chief Elizabeth Tilberis. Following her distinguished predecessors Beatrix Miller and Anna Wintour, she has produced a delectable, exciting magazine as appropriate and complementary to its moment as *Vogue* was at its very best in past decades.

I don't know who invented the fax machine, but he has earned my undying gratitude. When I worked on the first *In Vogue* I had permanent back-ache from carrying bound volumes home. In comparison, this was a doddle.

Contents

Preface

When Georgina Howell wrote *In Vogue* in 1976 it was British *Vogue*'s 60th Birthday. It was a very fine reference book. This new edition of *In Vogue* has been revised and brought entirely up to date. Now *In Vogue* is re-published and *Vogue* celebrates its 75th Birthday.

In 1976, I was a fashion editor in *Vogue*'s fashion room. I remember that the publication of *In Vogue* created a great stir and was a major triumph for Georgina. This was the book that filled the gap left when the great fashion writer James Laver put down his pen. It skilfully and successfully mixed fashion's changes and social currents, and its visual images were magnificent, drawn from 60 years of the magazine's archives.

So the 1976 edition of *In Vogue* did not disappoint. Through the following years I have constantly lent my now ageing copy to fashion journalists, students and editors. Its strong statements on fashion trends, its historical documentation and its clear views help both writer and stylist alike. Many, many times people have begged to find out where more copies are available, and *Vogue*'s art deparment's copy is labelled in gold for safe keeping!

Fashion has seen many changes since 1976. Georgina's writing reflects this and she has moved *In Vogue* into the 1990s with her instinctive style and understanding of social movements and fashion documentation.

It is now an even finer reference book.

Elizabeth Tilberis
Editor-in-Chief, *Vogue*

Writing *In Vogue* taught me 20th century history the only way I can remember it: by the way people talked and stood and danced, what they said and read and ate, who they wanted to look like, what they wore and how they decorated their homes. *Vogue* has had its finger on the pulse of all that for 75 years, surviving war, recession and competition to reach a readership of over 1,619,000, including 300,000 men.

To flip through *Vogue*'s 75 years of icons and images is to watch society transform itself before your eyes. A dance-past of the women we wanted to look like would open with soubrettes and duchesses, pass through a second act of society girls and film stars and leave us with royalty, rock stars and - now that you can be famous for being famous - the fashion models themselves. The half of the magazine that isn't fashion is to be seen as a great gallery of photography, art and design. Enticing and challenging its readers on the fashion pages, on the features pages it has recently embraced AIDS awareness, black culture, green politics and the anti-fur campaign.

The secret of *Vogue*'s success has always been its unrivalled access. Its regular contributors in the twenties included Aldous Huxley, Nancy Cunard and Cecil Beaton, and it called in features by Virginia Woolf, Noël Coward, Jean Cocteau, Evelyn Waugh, D. H. Lawrence, Vita Sackville-West and the Sitwells. In the corridors of Vogue House in the sixties you met David Bailey, Mick Jagger, Elizabeth Taylor, Terence Stamp, Jonathan Miller, Jane Asher, David Hockney, Ossie Clark, Tom Wolfe. In the eighties you met Prince, Kylie Minogue, Calvin Klein, or the Princess of Wales using the backstairs lift: her sisters Jane and Sarah both worked on the magazine.

By employing the right mixture of classiness and talent - the latter through its annual contest - *Vogue* early developed a pincer strategy for capturing its prey, the name of the moment. The glittering ranks of the magazine's great photographers (Hoppé, de Meyer, later Cecil Beaton, Horst or Hoyningen-Huené, Lee Miller, Norman Parkinson, Irving Penn, Snowdon, Avedon, Bailey, Donovan, Bruce Weber or Herb Ritts and many more) have met on their own ground the contemporary ideals *Vogue* wanted to feature. Only *Vogue* could take its readers on honeymoon with the Duke and Duchess of Windsor, and backstage with Prince.

So when I was asked to write *In Vogue*, it would have been perverse to put together a book that stopped at changing hemlines.

Georgina Howell

The Great War changed everything: way of life, attitudes, society, politics, people themselves mentally and physically. No war had ever involved so many civilians. Fashion in clothes and much else was turned upside down and no longer flowed in natural progressions and reactions. With hindsight, we know that World War I emancipated fashion, but while it was happening the breeches of 'farmerettes' and land girls, the trousers and overalls of the women munition workers and tram conductors, the uniforms of the nurses and postwomen were not considered part of fashion and scarcely surfaced to the pages of *Vogue*. Fashion dawdled in its tracks and simultaneously hopped a decade. Some people assumed that after the war there would be a rush of exaggerated impractical clothes as a reaction to serge suits and sensible proofed trenchcoats, others that women who had once known the freedom of trousers would never look back. Both were right.

VOGUE

Condé Nast & Co.

Fashion didn't catch up with itself until the mid-twenties. In the meantime sports clothes and jerseys took women forwards, crinolines, pagoda hips and tapered hems took them back. The cross currents brought to *Vogue* perhaps the oddest silhouette in the history of fashion. A woman might wear a hat of vulture quills two feet tall, a calf-length dress under a tunic dropping two points to touch the ground, the whole swathed with a tempest of monkey fur bands. In the evening she might wear a brocade tunic over a sagging nappy of chiffon, or a short crinoline in tiers of fur and lamé.

inées that combined worthy war-work with society spectaculars. Lady Duff Gordon was photographed as 'the personification of the mystery and power of Russia' at the Ten Allies Costume Ball, Miss Fay Compton as a rose and Miss Viola Tree as a 'tall bramble' at the 'Our Day' matinée, Ethel Barrymore as Flanders at the Allied Nations pageant on Long Island. 'Dressing on a war income' was a regular feature, but not as helpful as it might have been, recommending that women should slim in order to use less fabric, and suggesting 'cleverly contrived neck arrangements' to

Coming out bang in the middle of the war, British *Vogue* was full of references to hard times and reduced incomes, but each issue was full of the fashion news from Paris. Under headlines such as 'Paris makes a brave show in spite of guns', or 'Paris lifts ever so little the ban on gaiety,' *Vogue* managed to show the most extravagant of morale-boosting fashions. Once or twice a year there would be a page on 'A wardrobe for the woman war-worker ... for the ten thousand women who are driving ambulances, working in canteens and nursing the wounded.' There were a few features on war topics: the Citroën munitions factory, an eyewitness's account of a night with a convoy, the new ambulances. *Vogue* recommended gifts for soldiers - horsehair gloves, air pillows and National War bonds - and gave much space to the charity mat-

change the look of a plain dress. In 1917 *Vogue* reported that the French government had banned jewels and evening dress at the Opéra, the Odéon and the Comédie Française until the end of the war and had appealed to the public not to buy new dresses, and showed on the same page Doucet's frivolous evening wrap of rose panne velvet finished with skunk and tassels.

There was a feature on Leave Trousseaux with adjuncts to 'make it (your) business to see that he carries away with him on his return to duty a refreshing vision of loveliness, and in particular to avoid the masculine', in other words the wartime innovations of 'service suits', waterproofs, wool underwear, thick stockings, tailored Viyella shirts, trenchcoats and suits of uniform cloth copied from the soldiers' coats of black rubber or serge.

Uniform and civies:
Miss Joan Campbell of
the Red Cross and
Molyneux' summer
outfit of black and white
with velvet parasol

THE first women to wear trousers and dungarees wore them because they went with the job - dirty, hard jobs that women were taking over from the soldiers: train driving, plumbing, factory work, electrical engineering, window cleaning, farm labouring. Working clothes weren't considered part of fashion at all, just a temporary necessity like uniform, and *Vogue* reflected the attitude with one or two pages a year on equipment for ambulance drivers, compared with the main body of Paris fashion in every issue. Nevertheless short skirts and trousers became part of the vocabulary of fashion, and two coat designs arrived that stayed for good. The British Warm became the standard overcoat for men and women alike, with its deep revers, its epaulettes and buckled belt. From the mud of the front line came the trenchcoat, just as useful for land girls or even commuters in taxiless cities. In rubberized cloth, it had double breasting, epaulettes and cuffstraps, an envelope flap across the shoulder fastening, and a button-on chin protector.

Society beauties had their portraits taken for *Vogue* by Hoppé, Hugh Cecil and Bertram Park. Ideally they were photographed in uniform, like Countess Bathurst in Red Cross outfit, or the Marchioness of Londonderry in the uniform of the Women's Service Legion. Failing that, they compensated in other ways. Mrs Kermit Roosevelt's caption refers to her baby, and the career of her husband at the Front. The Duchess of Wellington is photographed knitting a sock. Mrs Vincent Astor, photographed in a garden hat, has the intention of opening a convalescent home near Paris where wounded American soldiers may be nursed back to health. Lady Randolph Churchill 'has organized some very beautiful tableaux vivants for the matinée', and Miss Lucile Baldwin took 'active part, last autumn, in the Tuxedo Horticultural Society, which gave an exhibition for the Red Cross'. Musical comedy actresses and starlets did their bit, too. Lily Elsie appealed for cigarette papers for the Red Cross with a new photograph in *Vogue*, Doris Keane told *Vogue* she was going to put all her fan letters from soldiers into a book and sell it in aid of the Red Cross.

Vogue was packed with patriotic advertisements, all urging the public to spend money in the line of duty. 'In too many homes ... these are the times of the darkest clouds. Yet assuredly it is true, and the old saying is justified of its belief, that every cloud has a silver lining. It is the writer's opinion the bright relief is the keeping up of the home ... at Jelk's you can obtain the best furniture at the lowest prices.' There were appeals to women to think of their complexions: '... comes the remembrance of bitterly cold days when you were driving an Army Car, of hours spent in heated factories, and the wonder of what effect either has had on your complexion, hands and hair. Your mirror reassures you, Colleen Shampoos so soon restore lustre and life to the hair ...' or, in a higher tone, 'It is lamentable that the far-famed beauty of the Englishwoman must suffer from the terrible strain her beloved country is undergoing. It is her duty to use every means in her power to prevent the effect on her beauty ... You are urged to take one treatment at the elegant and most up-to-date "Cyclax" Salons.'

'How the dentist gets to Tommy': a mobile dental surgery, and, opposite, Countess Bathurst in uniform

THE soldiers came home from the trenches different men. Many were suffering from shell shock with nightmares and vivid daydreams, and if they recovered now they would probably go down with nervous breakdowns in 1921 or 1922. They were out of temper with Lloyd George and his Coalition government. They'd been promised a life fit for heroes at the end of the struggle, but they came home to an impoverished country in a state of confusion, and their jobs had been filled by women or men who had managed to avoid conscription. Officers, the husbands of *Vogue* readers, were given no unemployment benefits and high prices were followed by a slump. There was plenty to escape from.

Women had grown more confident, more independent, and had begun to earn their own living in factories and offices. They no longer wanted to be cooks, nurses, maids or dressmakers: as Dorothy Parker wrote in 1919, 'that sort of thing simply isn't being done, any more; it is considered positively unfeminine'. The war had killed one out of every seven eligible men, and seriously injured another, so marriage was not inevitable. Women were in better shape after years of rationed butter and sugar, and with the popularity of hockey and tennis. The hourglass figure of the old Gaiety girls now looked comic. Laced whalebone corsets had been superseded by camisole bras and rubber girdles. The flapper had arrived. The expression, which began as '*backfisch*' in Germany in the 1890s, had meant a very young tart before the war, but had come to mean the popular heroine of the munitions factory, a girl who rode on the flapper bracket of a motorbicycle, swore, smoked cigarettes publicly and sold flags with brazen flirtatiousness. This figure had little to do with the refined dignified dresses in *Vogue*, which regretted the fact in 1921: 'One cannot help wishing for a less independent, less hard, more feminine product than the average 20th century girl.'

The new society had a new etiquette. At the end of 1918 class distinctions were temporarily relaxed. An aristocratic woman might marry even into the labouring class as long as the man had a good war record. The 'new rich', the war profiteers, were hated by the new poor. Women were smoking in public, but the cigarettes had to be Egyptian and Turkish, not Virginian. It was considered all right to smoke in the restaurant car of a train, but vulgar on the top of a bus. Some women smoked in restaurants, and a waiter in one knocked a cigarette out of a lady's mouth. In 1919 new dance clubs and halls opened for tea dances, practice dances, subscription and victory dances. You could dance before lunch in private houses in London and the country. Before the war women danced the tango with hands on hips and pelvis thrust forward, faces white with rice powder, eyes blackened with kohl, called mascara. After the war they danced the kikikari or the shimmy with deadpan faces and a touch of lipstick, in a backless dress ... 'I wish I could shimmy like my sister Kate, she shakes it like a bowl of jelly on a plate.' A clergyman in 1919 wrote, 'If these up-to-date dances, described as the "latest craze", are within a hundred miles of all I hear about them, I should say that the morals of a pig-sty would be respectable in comparison.' *Vogue*, appealing to the mothers, found a tone of voice that combined tolerance with disapproval: 'a formal "coming out" seems to have gone the way of formal visits ... Personally, one may feel that too much ease is being used too easily, particularly by people for whom formality might have served in place of those traditions which they lack ... In any event, girls will grow up, bless them!' Debutantes in 1920 were sending out invitations in their own names to dances where there would be no chaperones. Girls were often invited to bring their own man.

Women's place was a debatable subject. As a reward for war services they were given the vote over thirty, but the government was counting on half the female population being too vain to give away their age, and the other half to put in 'safe' votes. 'From the princess to the humblest of munitions workers, the womanhood of Britain emerges from the ordeal with credentials which the future will acclaim,' but many of the women who'd been praised for going out to work to help their country had their jobs snatched back in peacetime by Trades Unions: the soldiers wanted their work back again. Where women hung onto their jobs their pay was two-thirds that of a man. 'Votes for Women' gave way to 'Equal pay for Equal work'. The Sex Disqualification (Removal) Act of 1919 admitted women to many professions including the bar, and was followed up by acts to recognize women as morally responsible persons. In 1921 *Vogue* published 'Women and Education - a real Oxford for women', to help appeal for funds for Oxford women's colleges. It was timed to accompany the announcement that the Queen would accept an honourary degree at Oxford. *Vogue* said, 'The women's part of the university will never possess the spirit which alone justifies Oxford's existence, until it has

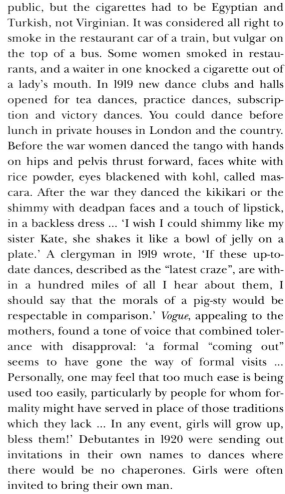

acquired the same freedom, intellectual as well as social, which characterizes the men's part.' Oxford had admitted women to full membership in 1919, but Cambridge had refused with scenes of amazing ungallantry, hoisting high above the streets a female dummy in bloomers riding a bicycle, and was consequently in disgrace.

In 1919 a terrible epidemic of septic influenza swept through Europe and on round the world killing 27 million people in all - twice as many as the war itself. In the United Kingdom there were 200,000 deaths, and people went about in public in antiseptic gauze masks. The dogs that accompanied them were muzzled, too: there had been an outbreak of rabies. There were high prices and strikes, pea-souper fogs, and precious little coal. Even if

your family were alive and together again, there were plenty of reasons for escapism and plenty to escape to. There was the light, bright note of the theatre - 'It will be a long time before the theatre can be serious again' - there was the cinema, there were cocktails and dancing, fancy dress balls, cabarets, weekend motoring and Fridays-to-Mondays. In summer families flooded to the seaside for their first holiday in five years: 300,000 visitors went to Blackpool, and women and children had to sleep in police cells while men slept out on the beaches and cliff tops. By the winter continental holidays were possible again for those who could afford them, and St Moritz was the place to go. *Vogue* ran a five-page feature on the right clothes to wear for skiing.

The new woman: the piquant Marie Doro, opposite, and the brazen new smoker as drawn by Benito, above

THE greatest influence of all on fashion was the great and continuing inspiration of the Russian Ballet. It was one consolation for the Russian Revolution that it had left half the Imperial Ballet permanently exiled abroad. Osbert Sitwell in *Great Morning* wrote, 'decoration was in the air ... the currents that showed were mostly foreign, and reached life through the theatre ... every chair cover,

every lamp-shade, every cushion reflected the Russian Ballet, the Grecian or Oriental visions of Bakst and Benois.' The barbaric beauty of the costumes and settings, the dancing of Karsavina, Lopokova, Pavlova, Nijinksy, Massine and the music of Rimsky-Korsakov, Balakirev, Debussy, Tchaikovsky combined in the most majestic and romantic of escapist fantasies. There was some doubt from

Vogue's theatre critic as to how one should react to them: 'There is really something a little incongruous in the Russian Ballet serving as a popular entertainment in a country which has begun to rage against wealth and leisure', and more doubts as to the audience's understanding of it: 'It is useless to pretend that the thousands who throng to see these ballets have the remotest idea as to what they really represent or signify.'

There was no fashion designer who had not been set off in a new direction by the Russian Ballet, but perhaps those most influenced were Poiret, who took the whole thing in at a gulp, Callot, Doeuillet, Lucile, Redfern, Idare and Chanel in her embroideries. Geometric prints, trellised and striped furs, silver and gold lace, brilliant linings, bead and silk embroidery, velvets and furs, boots, cockades and storms of feathers, glittering dragonfly lingerie and butterfly evening dresses with trains and wing sleeves, all that was most beautiful and extraordinary in Oriental fashion came straight off Diaghilev's stage. Until his death in 1929 there was nothing on the stage to rival the excitement his seasons aroused, although the original company had long since dispersed. The ballerinas naturally appeared very often in *Vogue*, and the next generation of dancers that had learnt from them: Mlle Rambert, who had learnt eurhythmics with Jacques Dalcroze and classical ballet with Nijinsky, and Madame Donnet, who founded the Ballet Philosophique. The passion for every kind of dancing was in the air. *Vogue* showed the schools of Marian Morgan, opposite left, and Margaret Morris, opposite below, and photographed Isadora Duncan in America, with barefoot Woodland Dancers 'all born in Arcadia' responding freely to the open fields and sky.

In violent reaction to hard times and sensible

clothes, the longing for escape and glamour brought a wave of fantastic fashion follies into *Vogue*. The theatrical came into the forefront of fashion. The modern woman in the gaiter suit turned into a beautiful barbarian in the evening, in a costume that might have been designed by Bakst. All Paris came out with evening dresses in tiers of shot tulle or silver lace and tea-rose brocade, with Turkish trousers of looped chiffon, lamé jackets, wings and trains of sparkling chiffon, turbans and fountains of ostrich feathers. Lucile's evening dresses, négligées and tea gowns were hardly different from her designs for the Ziegfeld Follies, and *Vogue* was filled with Egyptian gandouras, Caucasian waistcoats over dresses of metal bead embroidery, chains of gold and nets of pearls, butterfly sleeves of golden gauze, earrings dropping to the breast and headdresses of shooting feathers. Oriental tea gowns, originally made to be worn between hunting and dressing for dinner, were worn now for informal dinners. Ida Rubinstein's dress by Worth looked like the saris of the Indian dancer Roshanara - who turned out to be English. The Oriental influence came to an end in 1923 with a splendid 'Chinese Ball' in Paris, the French couturiers competing to dress the leading society figures.

IF the greatest single influence on fashion was Oriental, the second was American. Both were enjoyed as a relief from wartime problems and restrictions. The prestige of America was never higher. The States had lost one-fiftieth of proportionate British losses in the war, yet had the glory of deciding the issue and bringing an end to the struggle. America came out of the war richer than before, whereas France and Britain were impoverished, Germany bankrupt, Austria destitute. Americans gave the lead in all social fashions, and brought jazz, films, coloured nail polish, rouge, cocktails, smoking and money into Europe. British *Vogue* was full of American social life, American cars, Venetian palaces erected in Florida, American architects' houses, American resorts. Tourists from all over the States arrived in Britain from 1919 to buy up books, art, and sometimes houses wholesale. Agecroft Hall

in Lancashire and Great Lodge in Essex were transported brick by brick and rebuilt in America. In return we got syncopated music, and what to do to it - the Baleta, the Maxina, the Twinkle, the Jog Trot, the Vampire, the Missouri Walk, the Elfreda. These new dances were practised in the restaurant-clubs that opened when the Licensing Act of 1921 allowed people to drink and dine at the same place. There was the Kit-Cat Club where you might see the Prince of Wales, the '43 where you might see Augustus John, Carpentier the boxer, or Chang the dope-gang king. To show how all the new dances should be done there were the Castles, Americans naturally, the first of a line of polished dancing couples that would include Maurice and Leonora Hughes, and Fred and Adèle Astaire. The Castles danced in hotels, cabarets and private soirées as well as on the stage. Mrs Vernon Castle, below left, beautiful, vivacious and chic, appeared countless times in *Vogue*, lending her charm and elegance to fur coats, tennis dresses, riding habits, evening dresses, wedding dresses and every shape of hat.

Whatever was a source of inspiration and energy in any field was caught and turned into fashion in Paris - even when in 1923 Lord Carnarvon discovered the unrifled tomb of Tutankhamen at Luxor, and Ancient Egypt suddenly became fashionable. From 1916 to at least the mid-twenties the most important feature in any issue of *Vogue* was the Seen in Paris fashion lead, and it was the great French designers whose clothes were drawn, photographed in the Bois, and seen on actresses, film stars and socialites the world over. Nine of the couture houses had kept open during the war, even presenting their collections while Big Bertha was showering the city with shells, or when the guns were audible not fifty miles away. Clothes were generally shown on mannikins, and in 1918 *Vogue* wrote, 'We were amused because the mannikins wore hats which were selected to suit their dresses, and consequently looked like real women of the world whom one might meet on a walk in the Bois.' Women ordered their clothes from sketches, or from examples shown on inanimate figures, and it was a great advance in 1919 when houses began to show their clothes on women who walked and turned around to demonstrate the look in action.

Best-established couture houses in Paris during the war were Worth, Doucet, Lanvin, Paquin and Poiret. Charles Frederick Worth had set the pattern for the *haute couture* by becoming dressmaker to the Empress Eugenie. He made for her the crinolines we see in Winterhalter portraits, the first ever tailor-made suit, introduced the train and then the bustle. His house carried on with splendid and luxurious fashion. Jacques Doucet, who trained Poiret, made restrained and elegant clothes, and was a connoisseur and patron of the arts. He was one of the first to buy paintings by the Impressionists, Picasso, and to collect Negro sculpture. Paul Poiret burst onto the scene in the first decade of the century, a megalomaniac, a dazzling designer of theatrical costume, and an inconsistent fashion dictator who urged women to abandon corsets on the one hand and on the other threw a lassoo round their ankles, in the form of hobble skirts. Trained by Doucet, he dressed Ida Rubinstein, Isadora Duncan, Eleanora Duse, Sarah Bernhardt, and in 1919 was making a comeback after a disastrous war: a law had to be passed specially for his benefit, forbidding soldiers to design their own uniforms. As the twenties approached his importance waned: he was never quite able to translate what was successful on the stage into clothes in which post-war women would be comfortable. He was the first couturier to launch perfumes and

for lace blouses and silver and gold lamé evening dresses, and had to their credit trained Madeleine Vionnet, perhaps the greatest of all the designers mentioned yet, who was a kind of architect of fashion. She designed a unique dress for each woman rather than a look, studying the client's proportions first on a wooden mannikin made to the exact dimensions. She chose the fabric and the line for the client's looks and character, and then cut with a mathematical precision. She invented cutting on the bias which changed the fit of clothes forever. Her clothes looked nothing off, but came to life on the body. She only enjoyed dressing beautiful women, and didn't even care to dress herself particularly well: 'I was always short and I hate small women.' Her favourite client was the most elegant woman in Paris, the Duchesse de Gramont.

Gabrielle Chanel was the other great designer whose influence still affects fashion today. From a poor family, she cut up her aunt's curtains to dress a doll, and grew up into a designer with an instinct for what was just about to happen in fashion. A realist, she came up with just the thing people wanted to wear time and time again. 'Chanel' came to mean a whole look from sailor hat down to beige and black slingback shoes, even the scent in the air. She opened a millinery shop in the rue Cambon, nursed in a Deauville hospital during the war, and opened her own boutique afterwards. She made jersey chic in simple grey and navy dresses that were quite unlike anything women had worn before. She made blue pullovers and pleated skirts for the women who were replacing men in offices and factories, turned sports

Into the twenties: plumed velvet hat by Molyneux, above left, and black and white dress by Lanvin, above right, both 1923

open a house for interior decoration; he initiated live models for fashion shows, the sunken bath, nail polish in Paris, and the private bar.

Jeanne Lanvin's reputation was made by the clothes she designed for her daughter, who became Comtesse de Polignac. Her love of Botticelli, stained glass windows and Impressionist paintings was reflected in her romantic clothes. She dressed the Princesse de Lucinge and Sasha Guitry's four wives.

Madame Paquin dressed the Queens of Belgium, Spain and Portugal and the queens of the *demi-monde*. A good businesswoman, she was elected chairman of the *haute couture* of Paris. Her contemporaries the Callot sisters introduced the fashion

clothes into everyday clothes, made trousers elegant, and gave costume jewellery an intrinsic value of its own.

In London there were branches of Worth, Redfern and Paquin, there was Reville & Rossiter, and there was Lucile, the only famous house which made clothes specifically for smart London life. Lady Duff Gordon ran her Lucile establishments in London, Paris, New York and Chicago. She closed the Paris branch during the war, returning from America to reopen in 1918. The sister of Elinor Glyn, she trained Molyneux. Lucile dresses were Oriental arabesques, dragonflies, pure enchantment: they were leisure clothes for escapists.

By 1920, the woman they dressed had a different shape. The hourglass figure from before the war had changed into a suppressed bosom and a slimmer, straighter torso. Pre-war underclothes had consisted of a bust-to-thigh whalebone corset with suspenders laced up over a drawstring shift and French drawers, and they were worn from the age of thirteen. After the war, with its shortages of butter and sugar, its work at the factory, its hockey and tennis, this was gradually simplified to a shapeless camisole bra and a girdle which reached from just above the waist to cover the hips. An American tourist in London was heard to say, 'Men won't dance with you if you're all laced up', and there were plenty of dances you couldn't do in corsets.

A great decade for fashion illustration: Lepape's one-shoulder décolletage, above, and Helen Dryden's bathing suit, opposite

A curious anomaly in the simplified state of underclothes were the bathing suits worn right into the middle of the twenties - elaborate wrapover jersey dresses and baggy pants to the knee, or petal skirts and embroidered knickerbockers, worn over a brassière-cum-corset in rubber sheeting, with a turban on the head.

Sports clothes were the thin end of the wedge in making all kinds of fashion easier to move and work in. Comparing the elaborate fantasies of evening clothes with the pullover and pleated skirt of the golfer, or the cotton smock with trousers of the gardener, it's difficult to realize they were contemporary. Out of sports clothes came a garment which women could make at home, and which became the bread-and-butter fashion of the British - the jersey. It

was new in 1919, and by the following year everyone had it: men soon followed with pullovers. These brisk and businesslike fashions, rather than the romantic extravagant ones, showed the direction of fashion for the following decade.

Women's looks had changed, too. '... and I heard, though I did not, myself, witness this,' reported *Vogue* in 1919, 'that during luncheon, at a well-known restaurant recently, a mutual friend of ours - it is not necessary to mention any name - was seen, not only to powder her nose in full view of everybody, but to redden her lips!' During the war, most women wore a touch of powder and a little eyelash dye, but nothing more until American tourists began flooding into Europe after the war, bringing with them lipstick, rouge, mascara and eyebrow pencil. Poiret was the first couturier to market his own scents and cosmetics: powder, lotion, cream, talcum, coloured nail polish, make-up base, rouge, eye shadow and stage make-up, but these were ahead of their time. Barbara Cartland describes herself in 1919: 'fair hair fluffed over the ears ... red lips, subject of much criticism and many arguments, and a clear skin helped by chalk-white face powder. There were only three shades obtainable, dead white, yellow and almost brown!' The important beauty houses of Elizabeth Arden, Cyclax and Helena Rubinstein were among the first to advertise in British *Vogue*, but their products were complexion creams, not yet make-up.

Vogue's wartime issues showed a marked difference between the looks of musical comedy actresses and society ladies: women on the stage, particularly Americans, knew how to use make-up and weren't ashamed of wearing it. But everyone's hair, when photographed hatless, showed roughened, broken ends from too many permanents or too much marcel waving with hot tongs. Everyone wanted as much hair and as many curls as possible, and in 1917 *Vogue* showed a page of London actresses in the style of the young ideal, Mary Pickford. The higher and higher hats needed a good cushion of hair for anchorage, and there were advertisements in every issue for postiches and toupées 'absolutely impossible to detect'. Henna was still the only reliable way to brighten the colour of your hair, for although peroxide had been used for ten years, its effect on the hair was difficult to gauge and dangerous to repeat too often. In 1922 beauty suddenly became a fully fledged business, with the first ever articles on beauty farms and electrical massage. As the slim silhouette took over, the emphasis was on sport and beauty exercises.

After the curls and the Grecian chignons that were part and parcel of the fashion for all kinds of big hats, the small fitted cloche brought in the bob, which became the 'shingle' or the 'bingle' of the twenties, and finally the Eton crop. 'My dear, your hair is too beautiful,' says a bobbed girl to her long-haired friend in *Punch*. 'You really ought to have it cut off.' The first bob appeared in *Vogue* in 1918, but this was two or three years before it became popular. By 1923 Benito was drawing a dozen variations of the same cut.

In 1923 *Vogue* showed the first sunlamp, as was to be found in the surgical wards of Princess Mary's Hospital - and a healthy tan began to be fashionable.

OF all escape valves, the films allowed you to live vicariously with the least effort. By 1919 half the population of Britain went to the pictures twice a week. Charlie Chaplin, who had been slated by the British press in 1915 as a young Englishman who was not doing his bit, was on everywhere, with Mary Pickford, whose baby ringlets and childish prettiness were much copied. Her antithesis was wicked wicked Theda Bara, epitomy of vamps, an aggressive *femme fatale* launched on the first big publicity wave. She went to press interviews in a

white limousine with Nubian footmen, primed with what she had to say: her name was an anagram of 'arab death', her nationality was to be revealed as French-Egyptian - she was really a Miss Goodman from Ohio. Her 'Kiss me, my fool' became a catch phrase. There was Clara Kimball Young, Tarzan's Jane, and sylph-like Lillian Gish, who starred in D. W. Griffith's *Birth of a Nation*, a four-hour film that consolidated the success of films as a new art form independent of the spoken word. She appeared in *Vogue* in 1918 in pictures from Griffith's war epic

Hearts of the World, filmed in France in the recently recaptured village of Ham. Most often in *Vogue* was Geraldine Farrar, a beautiful opera singer who signed up with Samuel Goldwyn at $10,000 a week: in 1916 *Vogue* showed stills from Cecil B. De Mille's 'photo-drama' *Joan of Arc*, in which she took the starring part. Norma Talmadge was in almost every issue, a teenage leading lady at Vitagraph who went on to manage her own film company. For ultra-escapism there was Gloria Swanson, who appeared in a Sennett comedy as early as 1916. She was sensationally fashionable in all her films: De Mille insisted on it. In films like *For Better For Worse* (1919) and *The Affairs of Anatol* (1921) she staggered under the weight of jewels, furs and ostrich plumes. *Vogue* considered her a prime example of movie bad taste, but she made a tremendous hit with the British public.

The subtitles to films brought American slang to Britain, and it was much relished and disapproved of: 'Beatrix Esmond goes nix on the love-stuff' and

Opposite, Clara Kimball, above left, Geraldine Farrar, and Florence Walton, above right

'You've dribbled a bibful, baby' were read out aloud by the audiences. *Vogue* wrote a piece on the murder of the English language. An American revue which came to London with Noël Coward in the cast had its name changed from *Oh Boy!* to *Oh Joy!*

The feeling that Hollywood was hardly respectable meant that only a few screen stars were included in the magazine, although everyone who was anyone in the theatre could be seen in *Vogue* constantly.

Paris set the fashion, and the musical comedy and vaudeville actresses from London, Paris and

Broadway wore the clothes to perfection. They were photographed as models if they were just beginning, as themselves when they'd arrived, and finally, when they were famous, in their own clothes from Callot and Poiret, Vionnet and Lanvin. Stars like Florence Walton and Gina Palerme were the staple diet of Paris designers. Yvonne Printemps took eighty Lanvins to New York, and Florence Walton was sent a Callot dress a week. *Vogue* showed drawings of many of them.

Except for a brief falling-off in audiences in 1921 when a coal strike turned theatres into refrigerators, the stage had never done better or set more fashions. Costume design for important productions was always undertaken by couturiers, so that theatre design was naturally absorbed into fashion and new productions were scanned for fashion pointers. *Vogue* showed the best stage costumes from Hindu dancers' to Poiret's extravagant Oriental designs for *Agfar* at the Pavilion. There were sentimental comedies like *Paddy, the Next Best Thing* which ran for three years, and *Chu Chin Chow* which ran for five. There was Ibsen for problem plays, Galsworthy and Shaw revivals, Oscar Wilde, Gilbert & Sullivan and *Charley's Aunt*. Birmingham repertory theatre produced *Cymbeline* in modern dress, with warriors in khaki. In 1923 Cochran brought Eleanora Duse to England for the first time in seventeen years and began a migration of foreign plays and players to London. There was Sacha Guitry's *Grand Guignol* season and Carel Capek's *R.U.R.* Somerset Maugham's *Our Betters* was too shocking, and *The Circle* was openly booed. Noël Coward's *The Young Idea* had only a short run in 1922. Public taste at this period was for something a little more sugary.

The first public appearance of *Façade* in 1923 brought the Sitwells into *Vogue* for the first time with a cautiously favourable review by Gerald Cumberland. Hidden behind a curtain painted by Frank Dobson, Edith Sitwell 'half sang, half shouted' her musical poetry through a Sengerphone. 'Her voice, beautiful in tone, full, resonant and clear, could, with effort, be heard above the decorative din of the music' by William Walton. This is Osbert Sitwell's own description of the reception: 'The front rows, especially, manifested their contempt and rage, and, albeit a good deal of applause countered the hissing ... nevertheless the atmosphere was so greatly and so evidently hostile that at the end of the performance several members of the audience came behind the curtain to warn my sister not to leave the platform until the crowd had dispersed.' The first book reviews in the magazine discussed David Garnett's *Lady into Fox*, Michael Arlen's *These Charming People*, D.H. Lawrence's *Kangaroo*, Clive Bell's *On British Freedom* and Vita Sackville-West's *Grey Wethers*.

If the actresses showed *Vogue* readers how to look in the new clothes, it was the society queens who personified fashion for the designers themselves. Beauties whose portraits appeared in *Vogue* and who really lived the life for which Paris fashion was designed were the Duchesse de Gramont (Madame Vionnet said that if she wanted to tell if a dress were right she had only to try it on the Duchesse); wealthy socialites Mrs Vanderbilt, Mrs Hatch and Countess Torby; Lady Lavery, a red-haired Irish-American from Chicago who married the painter Sir John Lavery in 1910 and became a well-known figure in London society. Her portrait was incorporated into her husband's design for Irish pound notes. There were the Duchess of Marlborough, the Queen of Spain, Lady Elizabeth Bowes-Lyon who was to become Queen, Princess Victoria, the Duchess of Sutherland, Mrs Dudley Ward who was seen everywhere with the Prince of Wales, and Mrs Ogden Mills, one of his hostesses in the USA.

Bridging the gap between aristocrat and popular figure, Lady Diana Cooper was the daughter of the Duke of Rutland, a Red Cross nurse from the war, and the star of Max Reinhardt's *The Miracle*. A

natural bohemian with a great appetite for life, she captured the public imagination, and her delicious blonde beauty together with the pastel colours she almost always wore were much copied. *Vogue* showed her portrait by Ambrose McEvoy, and her photograph taken by Bertram Park on the announcement of her marriage to Duff Cooper of the Grenadier Guards. Thousands of factory girls turned out to see her wedding.

Society life was much the same on both sides of the Channel, with lunches, art shows, theatre, concerts, cocktails, dancing, fancy dress balls, dinners. In London Dame Nellie Melba was singing at the Albert Hall, Madame Suggia playing the 'cello, John Goss singing, and Stravinsky performed at Wigmore Hall. According to *Vogue*'s critic the audience of society stars was full of 'poseurs and sycophants'. Under the headline 'Humours and Irrelevancies of the Nursery Music of Igor Stravinsky' he wrote, 'The first was a quasi-barbaric dance, only a few bars in length, but long enough, or short enough, to make people smile openly; at the second people laughed; at the third, a very solemn and ominous composition, people laughed still more.'

Below left, Mrs Ogden Mills, below right, Lady Lavery, and, opposite, Lady Diana Cooper

VOGUE's reception of contemporary painting was far from adventurous. Modigliani, Matisse, Picasso and Vlaminck were found 'disappointing', but clearly worrying. 'Wanted,' wrote the critic, 'a revival of national art. The artists ... foregathered in their little coteries, apart from the world, ply their esoteric mysteries more and more out of touch and sympathy with the great heart of the people,' and he concluded, damningly, 'The ultimate standard of art must be the breadth of its appeal.' He turned with relief to Sickert: 'One is glad and grateful to have been given this opportunity to study the work of one of the most honest, original and talented of English painters.' *Vogue* showed two wartime etchings of Nevinson, *Flooded Trench on the Yser,* left, and *1914*, below, Nevinson remarked, 'the public is more interested in the war than it is in art.' All the leading painters and sculptors appeared in *Vogue*, and the more academic their approach the better reviewed they were. For the guidance of readers, *Vogue* produced a humourous guide illustrated by Fish, 'Shining at a Private View', opposite: suggested useful phrases were 'What rhythmic movement!' 'What green! What red! What yellow!' or failing anything else, 'How very brave.' Marie Laurençin, Laura Knight and Nina Hamnett were the women painters *Vogue* preferred, and Marie Laurençin was to draw covers for the magazine in the 1920s. In the field of applied arts, furniture from the Omega Workshop was shown, simple chairs and chests painted in confused colours described by a contemporary as being 'like a dragon's miscarriage'.

29

By 1924 all the people had arrived, and the party was under full steam. It roared on until 1929, and expired with a Crash, leaving the guests bewildered and hung over. So much had happened in those six years, and ended so abruptly, that only a couple of years later the period seemed as distant as the days before the war. It is remembered as the Gay Twenties, the Roaring Twenties, but for the people who hadn't been asked to the party, nine-tenths of the population, it was a time of despair with hunger marches, dole queues and war heroes reduced to selling matches on the street. The undergraduates who rushed to man the buses and trains in the General Strike didn't know or care that the miners were striking for more work so that they could feed their families. There was a great distance between opposites which intensified

the gaiety of the party-goers, the intolerance of the establishment and the misery of the working class. Meanwhile the twenties in *Vogue* are a rich cocktail of society, the *avant-garde* and popular jazz, Hollywood, reportage and criticism. The regular contributors included Aldous Huxley and Nancy Cunard, Clive Bell and Cecil Beaton, and called in features by Virginia Woolf, Noël Coward, Jean Cocteau, D. H. Lawrence, Evelyn Waugh, Vita Sackville-West, the Sitwells, and many more. *Vogue* extended its territory, and found an energetic style quite different from the tone of its first decade. The pages looked ten times more interesting with photographs by Steichen and Hoyningen-Huene, Man Ray and Beaton, and came alive with subjects as different as Gertrude Stein - 'Certainly the union of oxygen with ostriches is not that of the taught tracer' - and the rhythms of the *Revue Nègre.*

EVERYTHING in the twenties was done after a cocktail, to jazz. How should a cocktail be drunk? 'Quickly, while it's still laughing at you,' replied Henry Craddock in the *Savoy Cocktail Book.* You bought the ice from the fishmonger for a shilling a lump, tied it up in a tea cloth and bashed it to bits on the floor. There was soon a cocktail shaker in every middle-class house, and *Vogue* showed designs for a private cocktail bar ... 'Planning a Gay Corner Devoted to the Shaker, the Cherry and the Row of Happy Bottles.' Before the war you drank nothing until you sat down for dinner, but now there were dry Martinis, Side-cars, Bosom Caressers, Manhattans, Between the Sheets, or gin-and-ginger-beer. Marcel Boulestin, the famous restaurateur who wrote about food for *Vogue*, remarked, 'Cocktails are the most romantic expression of modern life ... but the cocktail habit as practised in England now is a vice.'

In the morning, at tea time, and all night long people danced. The Prince of Wales kept a band playing for an hour and a half without a break while he one-stepped and Charlestoned with Mrs Dudley Ward. Barbara Cartland described how Friday-to-Monday guests in the country would start dancing to the gramophone as soon as they arrived, hurry upstairs to dress, drive fifteen or twenty miles to a dance or a hunt ball and dance until five in the morning. In London you went to a *thé dansant* at the Savoy for five shillings, or twenty other places for less, and after the theatre you would take a taxi to the Berkeley, the Mayfair or the Embassy and dance again to the music of the Savoy Orpheans, Le Roy Allwood or Ambrose. When you tired of hotels there were nightclubs, but if your favourite nightclub had just been raided and closed down, there were still bottle parties, respectable at first, random later, where there would be a Negro band and possibly a cabaret.

Cars had a tremendous romantic appeal in the twenties, the appeal of speed, powerful machinery and status symbol rolled into one. Michael Arlen summed it up in this description of Iris Storm's car in *The Green Hat*: 'Like a huge yellow insect that had dropped to earth from a butterfly civilization, this car, gallant and suave, rested in the lowly silence of the Shepherd Market night. Open as a yacht, it wore a great shining bonnet, and flying over the crest of this great bonnet, as though in proud flight over the heads of scores of phantom horses, was that silver stork by which the gentle may be pleased to know that they have just escaped death beneath the wheels of a Hispano-Suiza car.'

In Piccadilly, opposite, afternoon tea outfit by Maison Ross, with Invicta car. Chauffeur's uniform from Harrods. On the Riviera, above, Lelong's resort pyjamas, 'L'Heure Divine', at a beach bar. For Cowes week, right, Chanel outfits with Reboux hats

JAZZ in the early twenties meant 'heavily punctuated, relentless rhythm, with drums, rattles, bells, whistles, hooters and twanging banjoes'. By the time Aldous Huxley wrote this description in *Antic Hay*, the saxophone and trumpet had been added: 'Sweet, sweet and piercing, the saxophone pierced into the very bowels of compassion and tenderness, pierced like a revelation from heaven ... More ripely and roundly, with a kindly and less agonizing voluptuousness, the 'cello meditated those Mohammedan ecstasies ... the violin admitted refreshing draughts of fresh air ... and the piano hammered and rattled away unmindful of the sensibilities of the other instruments, banged away all the time, reminding everyone concerned, in a thoroughly business-like way, that this was a cabaret where people came to dance the fox trot.'

Round and round went the dancers all over Mayfair, usually in fancy dress, women dressed as men, men as women, everybody 'terribly serious; not a single laugh, or the palest ghost of a smile. Frantic noises and occasional cries of ecstasy come from half a dozen Negro players ... Dim lights, drowsy odours and futurist drawings on the walls and ceiling.'

The 'Original' Dixieland Jazz Band, white musicians, had opened at the Hammersmith Palais as early as 1919, and there had been a lot of diluted jazz since, but in 1925 the real thing was seen and heard in Paris. It had already happened in New York, where socialites went into the fringes of Harlem to dance and watch, and Negroes were invited up to Park Avenue apartments to teach the Charleston and the Black Bottom. The first all-coloured show written, produced and acted by Blacks was *Shuffle Along*, on Broadway in 1923. Since then there had been *Runnin' Wild*, *Chocolate Dandies*, *Honey* and *Dover Street to Dixie*, and there was soon to be a King Vidor film *Hallelujah*, made in Hollywood with an all-black cast. The *Revue Nègre* was the first to come to Paris, and the audiences were almost knocked out by the waves of energy and the noise which engulfed them from the footlights. Josephine Baker in her frill of bananas became an overnight sensation. Nancy Cunard was ecstatic about the 'perfect delight ... of Josephine Baker, left, most astounding of mulatto dancers, in her necklets, bracelets, and flouncing feathered loincloths. The fuzz has been taken out of her hair, which shines like a dark blue crystal, as she yodels (the nearest one can get to expressing it) and contorts her surprising form through a maze of complicated rhythms.' Another *Vogue* writer called her 'a woman possessed, a savage intoxicated with tom-toms, a shining *machine à danser*, an animal, all joint and no bones ... at one moment she is the fashion artist's model, at the next Picasso's.'

A year or two later, when she'd opened her own nightclub in Paris, John McMullin went to interview her. 'She has come in without a wrap, and the length of her graceful body, which is light sealskin brown, is swathed in a full blue tulle frock with a bodice of blue snakeskin ... she wears an enormous diamond ring and a very impressive diamond bracelet. Her hair, which naturally grows in tight curls, is plastered close to her head with white of egg and looks as though it were painted on her head with black shellac. As she appears at the Folies Bergères, one is struck by her great decadence of line. When, for the finale, she wears only a diamanté maillot of tulle and red gloves with diamond balls hanging from the tips of her fingers, the effect is up to the wildest imagination of Beardsley.' She went everywhere in her Voisin car, painted brown and upholstered in brown snakeskin exactly matched to her own skin, accompanied by a maid, a chauffeur, and a white

Josephine Baker at the Champs Elyseés en route for Berlin

eskimo dog bearing on top of its head the red imprint of her kiss.

Josephine Baker was followed by Florence Mills and the Blackbirds. If Josephine Baker was a '*machine à danser*', Florence Mills was a poignant ragamuffin, all thin wrists and legs like toothpicks. All of a sudden everything black was the rage: black and white décor, Babangi masks, heads wrapped up in turbans, bracelets up the whole arm, jazz and all Negro dances, particularly the Charleston. 'In the 18th century we made money out of Negroes. In the 20th they make money out of us,' said *Vogue*. 'The Negro is at last coming into his own. The most distinguished art critics say his sculpture is better than that of Phidias; the musicians say he composes better than Beethoven; the dance-enthusiasts add that he dances better than Nijinsky; and the cabaret and music hall proprietors admit that he pays better than anyone.' The rhythms and characters of the Negro revue were beautifully given by the Mexican caricaturist Miguel Covarrubias, with captions by a Negro poet, Eric D. Walrond ... 'Nothin' - Ah don't care whut it is - can get mah boy excited. Nothin'! And talk about havin' a way with wimmin, ain't nobody can tell him nothin' ... He's a dressin' up fool, dat boy is, an' he sure's got luck with de high yalla ladies.'

The new Negro had entered, created by the jazz spirit of their own invention, and people had suddenly to make their minds up about 'niggers'. *Books for the Morning Room Table* reviewed Carl Van Vechten's *Nigger Heaven* about life in Harlem, and David Garnett's *The Sailor's Return*. Writing about the latter, Edwin Muir wondered whether 'relations between a sailor and a negress are a fit subject for art; whether the theme is not too fantastic to have universal significance.' *Le Village Blanc* was a controversial book by Joe Alex about a party of French shipwrecked off Africa and captured by a tribe that had once been forced to exhibit itself in an exhibition native village in Paris. The chief turns them into an exhibition white village for the amusement of the tribe, with a bar, a café and a beauty parlour. Meanwhile Carl Einstein had written the definitive book on African sculpture, *Negerplastik*, and the Cubists had already absorbed Babangi masks and Dogon sculpture from the 1922 exhibition of French colonial art.

No sooner was jazz accepted as thrilling and artistic than there began to be a tendency among popular musicians to claim the credit for white culture. In 1926 *Vogue* was writing, 'How far syncopated music derives from the Negroes is doubtful, but certainly they are its best interpreters,' and George Gershwin, well known for his *Fascinatin' Rhythm* and *Rhapsody in Blue*, arrived in London to say, 'Well, sometimes I have got an inspiration from Negro spirituals. But it is doubtful if they are Negro

Skiddle up skat!
Skiddle up skat!
Oh, skiddle up,
skiddle up,
Skat! Skat! Skat!

at all. Paul Whiteman says they are mostly old English tunes.' Showing how to dance to the new tunes, old English or new American, were Maurice and Leonora Hughes, and Fred and Adèle Astaire. The Astaires drew enormous crowds in Gershwin's *Lady Be Good* in New York and London, 'Adèle squealing like a toy steam engine ... Fred pat-a-flapping a proposal of marriage sans music', and Maurice Chevalier and Yvonne Vallée called their 1927 revue *Whitebirds* ... 'a non-stop attaboy Charlestonized paean to the birds and the trees and the breeze - a lunatic dash past Nature at 60 miles an hour ... if this man loves Nature, then all the nightingales will soon be drinking dry Martinis.'

Drawings by Covarrubias.
The jazz band and
cubist backcloth from
the New York musical
Processional

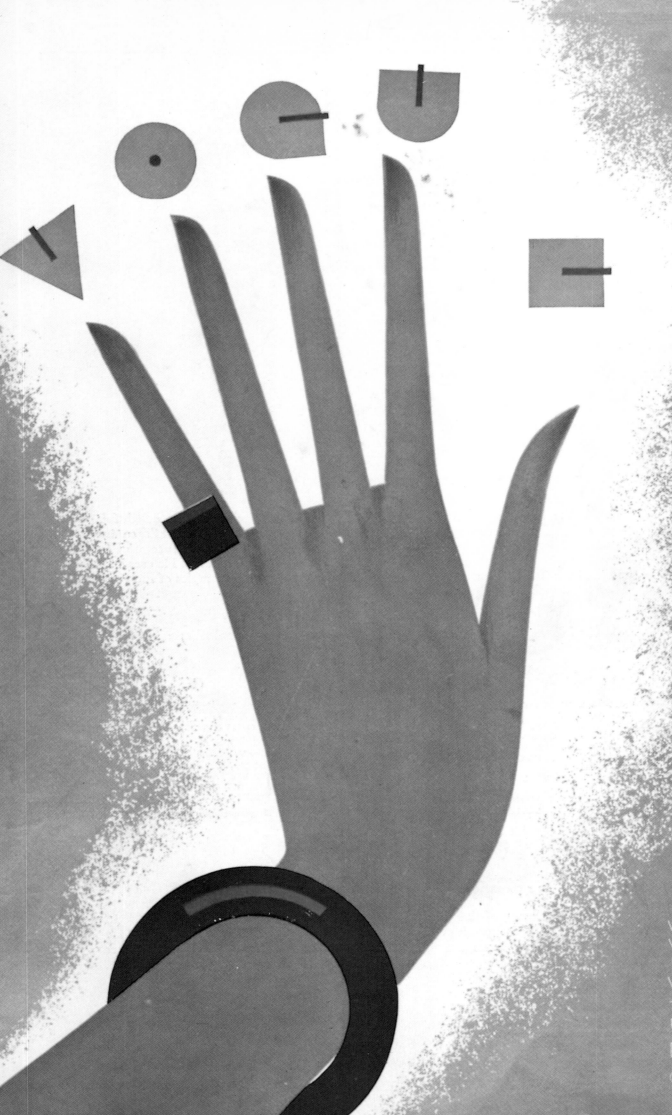

WITH FREE COUPON
VALUE 6ᵈ IN T
PURCHASE OF
VOGUE PATTER
THE CONDÉ NA
PUBLICATIONS
DEC·25·19
ONE SHILLI
(26)

VOGUE

WINTER SPORTS
NUMBER
INCLUDING A FREE COUPON
GOOD FOR 6° IN THE PURCHASE
OF ANY 2/- OR 3/- VOGUE PATTERN
The Condé Nast Publications, Ltd.
DECEMBER · 11 · 1929
ONE SHILLING
(25)

IN London gallery goers failed to see the point of much that was new in painting and sculpture. Clive Bell, writing in *Vogue* about Brancusi, complained, 'Within the last few months I have heard in London - in Paris, I think, that particular brand of imbecility is now known to be vulgar - the old familiar hee-haw, the fatuous comment, the time-worn joke, at the expense of one of the most serious of modern artists ... the fools approach and read in their catalogues *L'oiseau* or *Tête d'une femme*: peals of

In Paris, the Cubists, Expressionists, Futurists, Dadaists and the new Surrealists were not shut off in separate boxes. They were writing and making films, putting on plays, decorating and philosophizing. Many were involved in the ballet. Picasso had painted the famous curtain for *Train bleu*, shown in 1924 with costumes by Chanel, sets by Laurens and choreography by Nijinska, Nijinsky's sister, and designed for *Parade*, *Pulcinella* and *The Three Cornered Hat*. Matisse designed for Stravinsky's new one-act

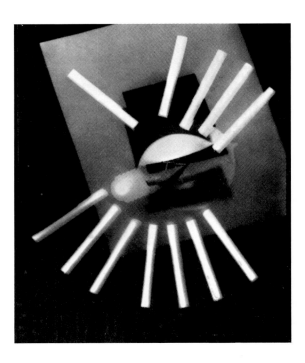

Picasso and Stravinsky by Jean Cocteau, above left. Man Ray's 'rayograph', 1925, above right. The children's escape from Fritz Lang's Metropolis, opposite: photograph of the scene being shot in 1926

laughter. Is it possible these oafs suppose that the sculptor was trying to make a photographic likeness of a bird or a woman, and could get no nearer than this? No: people who could suppose that are not allowed out.' *Vogue* had come a long way from the 1919 review that said, 'Art cannot flourish without a wealthy and leisured class to savour it - a class which has sufficient time and energy to refine its taste and to sharpen its intellect in social encounters.' And in the popular press, 'Mr Ben Nicholson has three muddy nudes against wishy-washy backgrounds. It is obvious that the figures are not meant to be anatomically probable - one woman's ankles are three times the width of her neck; one wonders simply why he had to paint them.' Even in 1929, Epstein's Rima was daubed with tar and feathers. In *The Long Weekend* Robert Graves and Alan Hodge pointed out that the public were slowly being educated into seeing things in an impressionistic or post-impressionistic way by fashion sketches and advertisements. In the Underground, and in *Vogue*, you could see posters by McKnight Kauffer, and because they were not in an art gallery they were looked at without prejudice or suspicion.

ballet *Le Chant du rossignol*, Braque for *Zéphyr et Flore*, Joan Miro and Max Ernst for *Romeo and Juliet*, and Marie Laurençin had designed some brief and modern costumes for Poulenc's *Les Biches*. In *Vogue* you could see Man Ray's mechanical experiments with film, composing photographs by exposing random objects directly to sensitive paper, and the latest work of Fernand Léger, key painter of the machine age whose pictures were composed like well-constructed aeroplanes or trains, in black and white with strong poster colours. The Surrealists' conference on sex in 1927 was ignored, with its relish for bad taste. The Surrealists savoured the *frissons* 'from the seduction of nuns and women who never washed, from outré sexual positions, from homosexual eccentricity'.

Jean Cocteau was a bridge between the arts, a gifted dilettante who helped initiate *Vogue* readers into the *avant-garde* by keeping three or four steps ahead. He had his first poems published at seventeen, and went on to write novels, ballets and plays, direct films, found a group of new musicians and publish his clever, tricky drawings. His one-act surreal tragedy *Orphée* was set in the technological present. Orpheus and Eurydice, in modern dress, confronted Death the operating surgeon with his two anaesthetists complete with rubber gloves, masks and surgical trolley. It caused some excitement, and *Vogue* called it at least the most interesting play of 1926. Another provocative play was Tristan Tzara's *Mouchoir de nuages*, with the actors sitting on stage, talking and making up, while the 'real' performance went on upon a small dais in the centre. This Roumanian Dadaist poet had staged the *Grand Spectacle du désastre* in 1920, which had succeeded only too well in rousing the audience to a pitch of fury.

The real centre of experimental theatre was Berlin. German Expressionism was an attempt to put a distance between the audience and the performance, to replace naturalism with stylization, to lose the individual in the mass. Characters were not given names, they were 'The Girl', 'The Boy', 'The Mother'. Bertolt Brecht said, 'I aim at an extremely classical, cold, highly intellectual style of performance. I am not writing for the scum who want to have the cockles of their heart warmed.' *The Threepenny Opera* was performed in 1928. *Vogue* summed up the social criticism of Sternheim and Wedekind and Toller as 'dramatized Freud', and gave the parallel movement in German dancing, with Mary Wigmar

leading her pupils in mass displays of gym and drill, the name 'tragic Tiller girls'. Berlin's favourite actress was Elizabeth Bergner, 'all nerves and delicacy', and Max Reinhardt, who turned crowd scenes into spectacular theatre all over Europe and America with Lady Diana Cooper's vehicle, *The Miracle*, was the key figure in Expressionist theatre.

Expressionism was most successful in German films, which were acknowledged even in Hollywood as technically excellent at a fraction of the cost of American production. By 1924 they had a stronger grip on the British film market than British films themselves. The movement kicked off in 1919 with *The Cabinet of Doctor Caligari*, a nightmare fantasy set in a fairground, written by Carl Mayer and Hans Janowitz and directed by Robert Weine. Material objects took on an emotional significance by means of clever photography and disturbing prop design: angles were acute, chimneys set aslant on roofs, and shadows were painted on to jar with lighting effects. By 1926 the most successful film in Berlin was a Soviet propaganda film, *Battleship Potemkin*. The story of a mutiny and massacre in Odessa, it was called 'a marvel of mass acting and machinery in

motion'. The same year *Vogue* published pictures of a new equally important film being made in Berlin, Fritz Lang's *Metropolis*, above, set in an underground city of the future with massed skyscrapers and terrifying machinery, and crowds surging through the maze in an attempt to escape from the flood.

That year Aldous Huxley in *Vogue* was criticizing Expressionist films for their pretentiousness and melodramatic ponderosity: 'A study of Felix the Cat would teach the German producers many valuable lessons.' He described how Felix sings a few crotchets, seizes them and fits them together into a scooter, an easy thing to do on film, an impossible thing to do in words, and draws an analogy with the super-realist writers. 'The fact is that these "young" writers are rebelling, not against effete literary conventions, but against language itself. They are trying to make words do what they cannot do, in the nature of things. They are working in the wrong medium. The aim of the super-realists is to free literature completely from logic and to give it the fantastic liberty of the dream. What they attempt to do - not very successfully - the camera achieves brilliantly.'

PARIS took the natural lead in all the arts except for films, and London followed. It was said the time lag in art fashions between France and educated England was about twelve years, and between educated England and the masses another two at least. Exhibitions held in the two cities in the mid-twenties summed up their relative positions. Wembley's Empire Exhibition was intended to enlarge the domestic market and encourage exports. Palaces of Art, Engineering and Industry jostled walled African towns, pagodas and Indian tombs; the Great Dipper was the steepest in England. King George V's opening speech was relayed by radio and between 6 and 7 million people heard his voice for the first time. Osbert Sitwell picked his way carefully through the sea of mud to pronounce the exhibition 'not ugly'.

In 1925 Paris opened the Decorative Arts Exhibition, the first on an international scale for over a century for which applied arts were the main reason. The exhibition gave its name to the style, which Osbert Lancaster called 'Modernistic' and 'Functional', and Bevis Hillier defined as including Erté ‧ on the one hand and the 'architectural nudism' of Le Corbusier, opposite, on the other. Inspired by Cubism, the Bauhaus and Aztec art, it took its rich colours from the Russian Ballet. Designs were intended for mass production in the new materials - plastics, ferro-concrete and vita-glass - and the aim was to combine art with industry. *Vogue* wrote, 'The Paris Exhibition is like a city in a dream, and the sort of dream that would give the psycho-analysts a good run for their money ... Enormous fountains of glass play among life-size cubist dolls and cascades of music wash down from the dizzy summits of four gargantuan towers.' Instead of the simpering dummies that were usually used for fashion exhibitions, André Vigneau had made formalized wax or composition figures, Modiglianis with sculptured hair. They were silver, red, purple or natural wood colour, and showed the new clothes off beautifully, although they were found '*quelque peu troublant*'.

Poiret, who had been impressed by design education in Germany and Austria before the war, and had founded his textile and furnishing house Martine on revolutionary lines in 1922, was naturally involved in the exhibition. He made a merry-go-round of Paris figures including an apache dancer, a *modiste* and a fishwife. He designed three barges which he called 'Love', 'Organs' and 'Delights'; asked why, he answered, 'Women, always women.' *Orgues* housed his new collection with wall hangings by Raoul Dufy, *Délices* was a restuarant, and in *Amours* Poiret sat playing a perfume piano, which fanned scented breezes at visitors when he pressed the notes for different scents.

THE Art Deco exhibition had an immediate effect on design, bringing a grisly period of 'traditional' copying to an end. *Vogue* included a *House & Garden* supplement in the magazine from 1924, and showed the new décor in detail. There were flats like Mrs Viveash's 'tastefully in the movement. The furniture was upholstered in fabrics designed by Dufy - of enormous flowers, printed in grey and ochre on a white ground. There were a couple of lamp-shades by Balla. On the pale rose-stippled walls hung three portraits of herself by three different and entirely incongruous painters, a selection of the usual oranges and lemons, and a rather forbidding contemporary nude painted in two shades of green.' *Vogue* showed the later school of all-white décor, pioneered by Syrie Maugham, with white leather chairs, Kakemono pictures, white damask curtains fringed with monkey fur, and bleached Louis Quinze commodes. Mrs Maugham stripped the leaves off lilacs and peonies so that they looked like wax flowers, and hired very black Negroes to play for her parties. Rooms were thought of, not so much to be lived in, but as settings for parties. Chelsea studios were taken over by 'Bohemians', who scattered cushions on the floor, made Batik prints out of balloon silk left over from the war, and played Mahjong after dinner. Big houses were turned into flats, wood was faced in mirror glass, and everything was disguised as something else. 'Gramophones masquerade as cocktail cabinets,' said Osbert Lancaster, 'cocktail cabinets as book-cases; radios lurk in tea-caddies and bronze nudes burst asunder at the waist-line to reveal cigarette lighters.' Duncan Grant and Vanessa Bell worked together to paint furniture and panels: *Vogue* showed their work in Virginia Woolf's house in Tavistock Square and Maynard Keynes's rooms in Cambridge.

Among the decoration, *Vogue* introduced the work of two architects who belonged fair and square in the machine age. Le Corbusier, who said, 'A house is a machine for living', designed rooms like operating theatres and buildings as severe as steamships. People who lived in his flats were allowed one picture, to be chosen from a picture-cupboard and changed as often as they liked. He believed that the construction should be clearly expressed in building, that kitchens and bathrooms should be given equal importance to drawing rooms and dining rooms. Eric Mendelsohn was a German architect, an Expressionist whose organic buildings looked as if they were whizzing along at a hundred miles an hour, swooping round corners. He could have been the original for Otto Friedrich Silenus, the architect in Evelyn Waugh's *Decline and Fall*, who had 'first attracted Mrs Beste-Chetwynde's attention with the rejected design for a chewing-gum factory', and replaced her country house with one of ferro-concrete and aluminium.

There was to be a sad difference between these romantic Futurist ideas and the cheapened versions that would be built all over Britain. Optimistic in 1925, *Vogue* was writing, 'In the future those who work in great centres will either live in garden cities, which will encircle London and Paris, or else in tall buildings reasonably close to the business quarters. The dreary suburbs will disappear ... it seems unlikely that most cities will increase in size. The Old World, at any rate, is greatly over-populated, and the size of urban populations depends eventually upon the size of fields upon which they depend for their food.'

Study and smoking room by Ruhlmann, 1925, opposite. Le Corbusier, above: 'a house is a machine for living'. Optical factory, below, by Erich Mendelsohn. House for an Englishman, right, by Professor Behrens of Vienna

THE right clothes to wear for the functional pavilions and machine-turned constructions of the Art Deco exhibition were Sonia Delaunay's. A Russian who came from St Petersburg as an art student, she arrived in Paris in 1900 and married the painter Robert Delaunay. Her patchwork dresses are pure colour kaleidoscoped together into vivid geometric and abstract designs, jumbled alphabets and mosaics. They were made for golf and Bugattis, and she had cars painted to match the clothes. She shared with the Vorticists and the Expressionists a romantic feeling for speed, fragmentation and the influence of machines. She made coherent compositions like living paintings, and wasn't interested in the draping of cloth. Her husband said that she 'possessed colour in its atavistic state' and her clothes inspired poems - Blaise Cendrars's 'On her dress she has a body', and Tristan Tzara's

> *L'ange a glissé sa main*
> *dans la corbeille l'œil des fruits.*
> *Il arrête les roues des autos,*
> *et le gyroscope vertigineux*
> *du cœur humain.*

The woman who wore these clothes, or clothes by Vionnet, Chanel, Molyneux, Louiseboulanger or the new Schiaparelli is perfectly described in *Antic Hay*: 'fairly tall, but seemed taller than she actually was, by reason of her remarkable slenderness. Not that she looked disagreeably thin, far from it. It was a rounded slenderness. The Complete Man decided to consider her as tubular - flexible and tubular, like a section of boa constrictor ... dressed in clothes that emphasized this serpentine slimness ...' The serpentine slimness was an essential. If dancing and tennis weren't enough, then you took tablets and potions, slogged it out on electric camels and did physical jerks first thing in the morning. You bought rubber rollers with studs all over them, you went to Baden-Baden, or best of all you went down to the Riviera and took instruction from a dazzling 'professor' of physical fitness. *Vogue* was full of pictures of princesses standing on their heads in pyramids, duchesses turning cartwheels and comtesses walking on their hands. Skirts and hair got shortest of all in 1926, and bosoms were compressed with 'flatteners'. Bathing costumes were designed with swimming in mind, and the boiling summer of 1928 put the seal on the craze for sunbathing and getting a tan. Naturally there were many criticisms of the new woman. *Vogue* warned in 1924 that 'a siren with a "stinker" between her lips does not inspire an epigram or

a lyric', but in 1928 Cecil Beaton was writing in the magazine, 'Our standards are so completely changed from the old that comparison or argument is impossible. We can only say, "But we *like* no chins! Du Maurier chins are as stodgy as porridge; we *prefer* high foreheads to low ones, we *prefer* flat noses and chests and schoolboy figures to bosoms and hips like water-melons in season. We like heavy eyelids; they are considered amusing and smart. We adore make-up and the gilded lily, and why not? Small dimpled hands make us feel quite sick; we like to see the forms of bones and gristle. We flatten out hair on purpose to make it sleek and silky and to show the shape of our skulls, and it is our supreme object to have a head looking like a wet football on a neck as thin as a governess's hatpin." ' English girls who looked like this were handed a giant bouquet by a member of the suite of King Amanaullah of Afghanistan who visited London in 1928. He told the *Daily News*, 'Look you, your English maidens are divinely beautiful, they are as fair as the pale moon which shines so gloriously in your western sky; their eyes are as bright as the eastern stars; and their complexion is just like the exquisite rose of Afghanistan.' That's what the reporter said he said, anyway.

The slim, brief look of twenties fashion was aided by the development of the artificial silk industry. Rayon printed well, it was light and cheap, and its production in the United States rose from eight million pounds weight in 1920 to fifty-three million in 1925. By then everything a woman wore could be cut out of seven yards of fabric, and rayon stockings were cheap enough for almost everyone. Unlike the early art. silk stockings, these went right up the legs to the thighs, and came in sunburn colour, not just black and white.

Jersey bathing suits, cotton bathrobes and silk bathing sandals, opposite and top right. Tourists in Morocco, top left, dressed by Jean Patou. Madam Agnès, bottom left, the Parisian milliner, in Futurist dress and earrings, 1925. Lee Miller, bottom right, in Chanel jersey, hat by Reboux

IN England, there were three schools of writing, described by Ronald Blythe in *The Age of Illusion* as Bloomsbury, Mayfair, and the leafy Blankshire of Georgian Poetry, where few people went any more: Bloomsbury was the withdrawn and aristocratic drawing-room world of Lady Ottoline Morrell, left, and the Woolfs, Clive and Vanessa Bell, Maynard Keynes and Lytton Strachey, with E. M. Forster on the perimeter. Mayfair, fabulously witty and irreverent, included Evelyn Waugh and Cyril Connolly. Still, for many readers, there was no writer like a dead writer and with this in mind Auden dedicated his *Poems* to Isherwood in 1930 with the words:

> *Let us honour if we can*
> *The vertical man*
> *Though we value none*
> *But the horizontal one.*

T. S. Eliot, below right, was one vertical man who was honoured and valued by contemporary writers. 'The Waste Land', written in 1922, acted as a catalyst. It had a note of gay disillusion and cynicism which they recognized as the mood of the decade:

> *When lovely woman stoops to folly and*
> *Paces about her room again, alone,*
> *She smoothes her hair with automatic hand,*
> *And puts a record on the gramophone.*

Much of his work was a great deal more difficult. He said, 'genuine poetry can communicate before it is understood', and 'the poet is occupied with frontiers of consciousness beyond which words fail, though meanings still exist'. In Paris, Gertrude Stein was making connections between words as words, explained to *Vogue* readers by Edith Sitwell, who made poetry fun.

> *With the flag.*
> *With the flag of sets.*
> *Sets of colour.*
> *Do you like flags.*
> *Blue flags smell sweetly.*
> *Blue flags in a whirl.*
> *The wind blows*
> *And the automobile goes.*

> '*... Flags make her think of irises. Flags make her think of the wind. The wind makes her think of the speed of automobiles.*'

James Joyce was more difficult than anyone. *Ulysses* had been published in 1922. Virginia Woolf wrote of 'a queasy undergraduate scratching his pimples', but T. S. Eliot said, 'How could anyone write again after achieving the immense prodigy of the last chapter?' Joyce said he had 'recorded, simultaneously, what a man says, sees, thinks and what such seeing, thinking, saying does to what you Freudians call the subconscious'.

The Sitwells, opposite: Edith, Osbert and Sacheverel. Lady Ottoline Morrell, above. Economist Maynard Keynes and his wife, right, the Russian ballerina Lydia Lopokova. Far right, T. S. Eliot

THE twenties gave women their freedom, sexually, through the work of Dr Marie Stopes and the setting up of birth control clinics, and politically. By the end of the decade the flapper vote had put 5 million more women on the electoral roll, which helped to bring in the second Labour government, fighting on unemployment. But it was not a political decade.

> *Ain't we got fun?*
> *Not much money, oh! but honey!*
> *Ain't we got fun?*
> *There's nothing surer,*
> *The rich get rich and the poor get - children.*
> *In the meantime, in between time,*
> *Ain't we got fun?*

Sexual deviation was becoming acceptable, at least by high society, due to the talent and gaiety of the homosexuals in the theatre and Mayfair, and due to the writers who put their predicament in readable form. 'And what is a "He-man?" ' asked Gertrude Stein. 'Isn't it a large enough order to fill out to the dimensions of all that "a man" has meant in the past? A "He-man!" ' This is how Scott Fitzgerald summed up the sexual education of the jazz age: 'We begin with the suggestion that Don Juan leads an interesting life (*Jurgen,* 1919); then we learn that there's a lot of sex around if we only knew it (*Winesburg Ohio,* 1920), that adolescents lead very amorous lives (*This Side of Paradise,* 1920), that there are a lot of neglected Anglo-Saxon words (*Ulysses,* 1921), that older people don't always resist sudden temptations (*Cytherea,* 1922), that girls are sometimes seduced without being ruined (*Flaming Youth,* 1922), that even rape often turns out well (*The Sheik,* 1922), that glamorous English ladies are often promiscuous (*The Green Hat,* 1924), that in fact they devote most of their time to it (*The Vortex,* 1926), that it's a damn good thing too (*Lady Chatterley's Lover,* 1928), and finally that there are abnormal variations (*The Well of Loneliness,* 1928, and *Sodom and Gomorrah,* 1929).'

The London stage barely went further than Noël Coward's *The Vortex,* which shocked playgoers because drug-taking had never been a stage theme before. *Vogue* said, 'to excite emotions of pity or anxiety a play must contain people who rouse the sympathy of the audience by intelligence or character. The protagonists of *The Vortex* had neither, and as a result in the last act, instead of being stirred by their efforts to reform, one wished the son would continue to take drugs and the mother lovers, till they both died: a good riddance to bad rubbish.' Coward, at any rate, loved the publicity and was photographed in decadent satin pyjamas telephoning from the futurist bed of his Ebury Street flat. His *Fallen Angels and Sirocco* provoked 'cries of "rotter!" from the stalls, cat calls and shrieks from the gallery', but by 1927 his good lyrics and catchy tunes, light touch and perfect timing had

won over audiences, and he had four shows running simultaneously. His leading lady, Gertrude Lawrence, below right, perfectly matched the brittle, disillusioned mood of his plays. Languid and sunburnt, with a smoky voice, she gave fashion the overworked word casual, wearing a mink coat thrown over flannel trousers. She looked perfect in Molyneux's spotted pyjamas or his white satin evening dress as she leant against the balcony and sang *Some day I'll find you.* 'She smoked cigarettes with a nuance that implied having just come out of bed and wanting to go back into it,' said Cecil Beaton. She had terrific style, and her arrival at the stage door was something worth waiting for, as she stepped out of her Hispano-Suiza with a corsage of orchids and a bevy of handsome young men with top hats and gardenias.

Bernard Shaw won the Nobel Prize for *Saint Joan* in 1924, with Sybil Thorndike in the lead. In the cast were Godfrey Winn, and Ernest Thesiger who left it for the new Cochran review. Cochran's Young Ladies were the best revue chorus of the day, and he was the leading showman and impressario of the twenties. He brought everything to London, from the Russian Ballet to a cowboy rodeo, from prize fights to cabarets.

A great draw of the day was Tallulah Bankhead, opposite, who attracted in particular enormous crowds of female fans - more than any matinée idol - who choked the West End and crammed around the stage door. Her ambivalent appeal and tough wit made her an essential at smart parties, though her remarks could be killers. At a wedding she might remark, 'I've had both of them, and they were

lousy', or at a first night, 'There's less in this than meets the eye.' She was a strange choice for Iris Storm in *The Green Hat,* Michael Arlen's successful novel made into a play. *Vogue* wrote, 'They take lovers as they take cocktails, and all the while use the words "clean" and "purity" as a chain-smoker uses cigarettes ... you cannot make *La Dame aux Camélias* drive a Hispano-Suiza' - and you certainly would not have picked Tallulah Bankhead to play a *Dame aux Camélias.* A powerhouse of energy and a great show-off, she was described by Cecil Beaton as 'a wicked archangel ... Medusa, very exotic, with a glorious skull, high pumice-stone cheekbones ... Her cheeks are huge acid-pink peonies. Her eyelashes are built out with hot liquid paint to look like burnt matches,

Early Cecil Beaton portrait of Tallulah Bankhead, opposite, here impersonating Sarah Bernhardt. Above, Bernard Shaw

Charles Spencer Chaplin,
as Vogue called him,
above, in 1926. Opposite,
the silent, solitary Garbo

and her sullen, discontented rosebud of a mouth is painted the brightest scarlet, and is as shiny as Tiptree's strawberry jam.' She never stopped talking, and a friend who once took out a stopwatch and counted her words per minute calculated that she spoke seventy thousand words a day - the wordage of *War and Peace* over a weekend. Emerging onto the street after lunch one day, she dropped a fifty dollar bill into the tambourine of a Salvation Army girl, and said, 'Don't bother to thank me, darling. I know what a perfectly ghastly season it's been for you Spanish dancers.'

Probably nothing gave so much pleasure to so many as the wireless. Everyone tuned in to the hour of dance band music in the evening, which left them

whistling tunes like *Bye Bye Blackbird, Valencia* or *I Wonder Where My Baby is Tonight.* But popular music programmes were few and far between, sprinkled among chamber music and symphony concerts. John Reith, the General Manager of the British Broadcasting Company, saw that the radio was potentially as important as the printing press in terms of human enlightenment, and felt it as a religious duty to keep the BBC free from commercialism and propaganda. The public resented their diet of musical education, as the press, and *Vogue*'s music columnist Edwin Evans, were quick to point out. They called him 'the Judge of What We Ought To Want', and he bleakly replied, 'I do not pretend to give the public what it wants.' It was due to him that the announcers wore dinner jackets to read the nine o'clock news, and the public began to enjoy excellent radio plays and the best musical performances.

For sheer entertainment you went to the cinema. Everyone loved Felix the Cat, Bonzo Dog, Mickey Mouse and the slapstick comedies with Fatty Arbuckle, the nightmare acrobatics of prim, shortsighted Harold Lloyd who was always suspended by a sagging flag pole over a dizzy drop, and the surreal machine-infested world of poker-faced Buster Keaton. Every successful film was followed by its burlesque, and the melodrama of Rudolph Valentino's films were a rich inspiration to Laurel and Hardy. Charles Chaplin, opposite, was still the most popular of all comedians, and *The Kid*, in which he adopts orphan Jackie Coogan, the most successful film of the twenties. Lon Chaney was Quasimodo in *The Hunchback of Notre Dame*, and it became a joke, when you saw a beetle scuttling over the floor, to shout, 'Don't kill it, it may be Lon Chaney in disguise.' Jim Tully told *Vogue* readers that Lon Chaney's father was a deaf and dumb Irish barber, that his mother was afflicted in the same way, and that he had learnt to mime by talking to them in sign language - a story that sounds as if it came from the press office. A quite different sort of film was a success in Britain when Robert Flaherty's documentary *Nanook of the North* was shown. About an Eskimo family, it showed how the camera could record domestic life without pretension or embarrassment.

The two big stars of the twenties were both Paramount properties, locked in a rivalry that made good gossip. Gloria Swanson arrived in Hollywood as a flat-figured extra from Chicago with brilliantined, spit-curled hair. Her camera-proof face, rather viciously beautiful, suited the most bizarre and exaggerated of fashions. She was a symbol of movie bad taste when she secured her social position by marrying the Marquis de la Falaise de Coudray, a 'docile nobleman with a reckless taste in spats'. She returned to her house in Hollywood and installed footmen in powdered wigs and satin knee-breeches.

Her rival Pola Negri, who was able to call herself Countess Dombski, was imported by Paramount because of her success in German films. She was overschooled by her studio, never caught on with the flapper fans as Gloria Swanson had, and was never very popular in Hollywood because she made no attempt to hide her contempt of American films and culture. She had some sort of affair with Rudolph Valentino, king of movie sheikhs and lounge lizards, and staged a dramatic fainting at his funeral that provoked more laughter than sympathy. She lost box office appeal towards the end of the decade and returned to Germany where, in 1936, she was once more starring in films and was rumoured to be a girl friend of Hitler.

Elinor Glyn's *Three Weeks* was a whale of a success, both the book and the film. A story about a Ruritanian Queen who enjoys three flaming weeks with Conrad Nagel on a bed of roses, it starred Eileen Pringle. Miss Pringle was reproved by the Deaf and Dumb Society who could see that when Conrad

Nagel swept her into his arms her lips were saying 'If you drop me, you –, I'll break your neck.' Clara Bow was the It Girl who invented sex appeal - *Flaming Youth* brought her 20,000 fan letters a week and made her everybody's sweetheart from 1925 to 1930. Sound came in in 1927, and by the end of 1928 the worst sound film could outdraw the best silent movie.

The greatest star of all arrived in the last years of the silent film. Greta Garbo, below, was nineteen when she came to Hollywood in the entourage of Mauritz Stiller. Daughter of a poor labourer, she was the lather girl in a barber's shop when she had begun to play extras in a few Swedish films. She was different because she didn't give herself titles or airs, and her relationship with M.G.M. and reporters was one of icy formality. She hated publicity, and only asked to 'be alone'. On the screen her amazing beauty overwhelmed the audience. She didn't have to act, her slightest gesture conveyed more than other people's words. When her first talkie, Eugene O'Neill's *Anna Christie* arrived in 1930, her fans sat on the edges of their seats. They were dying to hear her voice, said to be guttural and thickly Swedish. They sighed with relief, then swooned with delight: her first words were 'Gif me a viskey, ginger ale on the side - and don't be stingy, baby.' When her shoulder length bob and slouch hat began to be universally copied, it signalled the end of the twenties.

The Hon Mrs Reginald Fellowes, formerly Princess Jean de Broglie. Cecil Beaton said, 'she had the air of having just come off a yacht, which she very likely had'. In 1941 she would become the first President of the new Incorporated Society of London Fashion Designers

BY the end of the twenties fashionable restaurants could afford to spend £50,000 on redecorating, and cabarets brought in anything up to £1,000 a week. All the new restaurants and clubs were described in *Vogue*, and the people who went there. One of the smartest was the Kit-Cat where elegantly bored women looked over corsages of white orchids at cleanshaven young men with satin hair and wide shoulders: it was raided by the police the night after the Prince of Wales had dined there. Guests at Chez Victor, who crowded round the piano to hear Hutch sing *The Man I Love*, were appalled when Victor was convicted of breaking the Licensing Act and imprisoned. The Silver Slipper, with its glass floor and marvellous saxophonist, was the last big nightclub to be opened by Mrs Meyrick, who was imprisoned three times. Her clients over the years included a good cross section of twenties society, including Augustus John and Rudolph Valentino,

J. B. Priestley and Sophie Tucker, Carpentier the boxer and Michael Arlen. You could find Tallulah Bankhead at Taglioni's, Epstein and his latest model at the Ham Bone in Soho, John at the Eiffel Tower, and end up at the Gargoyle eating scrambled eggs and drinking coffee by an open fire. In the dancing room was David Tennant's huge Matisse, for which Lady Latham made some Negro art curtains. As *Vogue* said, 'Everyone agrees that with Matisse you can't go wrong.'

This was the heyday of hostesses, with Elsa Maxwell for their queen. She would take over a whole nightclub or palace in any capital city and fill it with her set of international celebrities. At her parties there was a touch of the grotesque: you might have to blow a feather off a sheet or milk an artificial cow for your champagne. Mrs Corrigan was an avid party-giver who conquered London society by the extravagance of her hospitality. The most sought-after guests would find that they had won the gold cigarette cases in the tombola, and the all-star cabaret got more for their brief appearance at Mrs Corrigan's than for a week in the theatre. Finally, Mrs Corrigan would stand on her head to a drum-roll. They said, 'The only sound at night is Mrs Corrigan climbing', but they went. This was Cecil Beaton's description in *Vogue* of a typical party of the time, given by Mrs Guinness: 'people literally overflowing into the street ... all the people one had ever known or even seen - up and down the big staircase, in the ballroom, along the corridors - "Hutch" singing in the ballroom while we all sat on

Circus parties, parties where one had to dress as someone else and almost naked parties in St John's Wood, parties in flats and studios and houses and ships and hotels and nightclubs, in windmills and swimming baths.' The swimming pool party given by Brian Howard and Elizabeth Ponsonby had a jazz band to which the guests danced in bathing suits. It caused a small scandal. The *Sunday Chronicle* wrote, 'Great astonishment and not a little indignation is being expressed in London over the revelation that in the early hours of yesterday morning a large number of society women were dancing in bathing dresses to the music of a Negro band at a "swim and

the floor - Edythe Baker playing to some of us in another room downstairs - Oliver Messel in the same room giving a ludicrously lifelike imitation of a lift-attendant describing the departments on each floor - Lady Ashley shining in a glittering short coat of silver sequins over her white dress - glimpses of the Ruthven twins - of Noël Coward looking happy and being amusing - Gladys Cooper in a Chanel rhinestone necklace that reached to the knees of her black velvet frock ... impression after impression, before one sank and sank ... to the supper room.'

Loelia Ponsonby, later the Duchess of Westminster, gave a different sort of party. She would ring up her friends at the last moment and ask them to come round with some food or champagne. Nine parties out of ten would be fancy dress. Evelyn Waugh in *Vile Bodies* wrote about 'Masked parties, savage parties, Victorian parties, Greek parties, Wild West parties, Russian parties,

dance" gathering organized by some of Mayfair's Bright Young People.' Brian Howard, down from Oxford, initiated 'Follow my Leader' through Selfridges, where a crowd of young people helpless with laughter tore about among the shoppers, jumping into lifts and climbing over the counters. Lord Bessborough and Prince Obolensky went to one of the Sutherlands' parties as drunken waiters, taking over from house staff, finally keeling over with a crash of breaking china. Lady Diana Cooper wrote, 'there was a fancy ball at Ava Ribblesdale's last night, and all the women looked fifty per cent worse than usual -S. as Little Lord Fauntleroy quite awful, P. as a street Arab just dirty.' It was a good time for twins, and there was a pair at every party - the plain but jolly Ruthven sisters, the Ward twins and the Rowe twins, Joan and Kit Dunn, or Thelma Furness and Gloria Vanderbilt, twice the woman for being indistinguishable.

The American decorator Lady Mendl, left, formerly Elsie de Wolfe. She brought the ruthlessness of a company director to the business of party-giving, with cross-filing systems to remind her what menus guests had already been given, and who had sat next to whom. Lady Diana Duff Cooper, right, 'untarnished, the loveliest young Englishwoman of her generation', a natural bohemian who could turn her hand to mechanics, diplomacy, farming and writing. Her role as the Madonna in Max Reinhardt's play The Miracle made her a heroine on two continents

Society in the twenties was large enough to be heterogeneous and international, but small enough for the prime figures to be well known to readers of gossip columns. It was a clever, amusing, worldly set at best, greatly improved by overlapping with the theatre and the new rich. The Prince of Wales gave English society its lead, and his friends were actresses and self-made men. London's theatrical peerage included Zena Dare who had become the Hon. Mrs Maurice Brett, Gertie Millar (the Countess of Dudley), Rosie Boot of the Gaiety (the Marchioness of Headfort), Beatrice Lillie (Lady Peel), and Lady Inverclyde, who had been June on the stage. The well-known beauty Lady Ashley was rumoured to be the daughter of an ostler. As Sylvia

The sauvage Baba D'Erlanger, above, and opposite, the ornamental Paula Gellibrand

Hawkes, her first job had been modelling at Reville, and she had been in the banned first London cabaret, 'Midnight Follies'. Her father-in-law, the Earl of Shaftesbury, was denying the engagement the day before the wedding, and none of the groom's family went to the marriage.

Society women were the new fashion dictators. They wore couture clothes and lived by the season - Deauville in spring, the Riviera in summer, Scotland in autumn, London and Paris in the winter. Fashion had become a matter of personal style, and the embodiment of the new style was Mrs Dudley Ward, who practised the Charleston with the Prince of Wales at the Café de Paris early in the mornings. Neat as a pin, she wore natty check suits with a clove

carnation and jingling bracelets, and dressed her daughters and herself to match in red gingham, with bows in the hair.

An exotic at the opposite end of the scale from Diana Cooper was Baba d'Erlanger, left, whose mother had brought her up to be highly unusual. As a child she had instead of a nanny a robed and turbaned mameluke, who followed her about like a page. The d'Erlangers lived in Byron's old house in Piccadilly, and gave marvellous children's parties to which Baba always wore gold. A *belle-laide* with a monkey face and scarlet lipstick, she became the Princesse Jean de Faucigny-Lucinge and set a fashion for wearing a tarbush cap and bunches of artificial fruit with a bathing suit.

The beauty of the moment was Paula Gellibrand, opposite, Baba d'Erlanger's best friend, a heavy-lidded Modigliani with a look of fatigue and sophistication. A golden blonde with enormous blue eyes, she glossed them with Vaseline, wore hats dripping with wistaria and got married in a dress as plain as a nun's habit. A *Vogue* model, she married an unusual man, the Marquis de Casa Maury, Castilian by ancestry, Cuban by nationality, English by education. He was an ace driver of a Bugatti in the Grands Prix, and the owner of the first Bermuda-rigged schooner in Europe, doing the navigating himself. When Wall Street crashed he built the Curzon cinema. He spent seven months learning the trade under assumed names, sweeping up, working the projector, selling the tickets, until he knew enough to make a great success of the Curzon.

Finally there was Mrs Reginald Fellowes, who invented the almost insulting elegance that was to be the ambition of model girls up to the 1960s. She loved making other women look silly, and usually managed it by looking much less 'dressed' than they did, arriving at greater elegance with far less apparent effort. She wore the same absolutely simple dress day after day, usually with a sequin dinner jacket and a green carnation. Actually the dress was probably a different one every night, since she ordered plain linen dresses in dozens. Meeting a woman in the same dress at a nightclub once, she called for a pair of scissors and snipped off her ostrich trimming. Her jewellery was remarkable: she had handcuffs of emeralds, necklets of stones brought to her from India, and conch shells made of diamonds.

So much had happened in the twenties, and so many new influences felt, that the change in fashion was bound to be radical. The people who wore the clothes overtook the designers, who were obliged by the middle twenties to conform to the uniform of short skirts, dropped waists and simplicity demanded by the lives and tastes of their public. The most important designers to emerge from the twenties were the two most involved with new movements in other fields - Chanel, whose circle included Picasso, Cocteau and Stravinsky, and the new Schiaparelli, whose friends were the Surrealists.

The thick skin that protected the rich and secure in the twenties wore paper-thin in the thirties. Groucho Marx called the years of American Depression before the New Deal the Threadbare Thirties, but the slump was an international crisis and in Britain the unemployment figures reached 3 million, and feelings of anxiety and insecurity were at their highest since the middle of the war. Owing to the decline of world trade and the collapse of markets, Britain was pock-marked with Distressed Areas where almost the entire population was living on the meagre dole. A policy of national self-sufficiency was reuniting Germany and giving it identity and a sense of purpose, but Britain was divided and on the point of crisis when the National Government was formed in 1931, and politics began to invade the lives and conversation of people who had never thought politically before. Hunger marchers poured into London by the thousand instead of the hundred, and demonstrations were charged by police with batons - in Birkenhead the street fighting went on for three days. As an economy measure, the National Government had introduced reductions in unemployment pay subject to the Means Test. A man would come round, notice a new coat or find out if a boy did a paper round, and cut the allowance. Men whose families could not live on the dole as it was faced cuts and deductions of food tickets. Sympathy for them caused a rift in the Labour party, and the Left was joined by university undergraduates and dissatisfied or sensitive elements of the middle and upper classes.

UNIVERSITY students who came out to see the hunger marchers spoke of the extraordinary sound of their feet, not marching like soldiers, but shuffling because of the flapping soles of their worn-out boots. In the twenties university students had rallied to the government in the General Strike. In the thirties they joined the marchers.

The situation was brought home to *Vogue*'s readership in other ways. Wal Hannington, organizer of the National Unemployed Workers' Movement, used the nuisance tactics exploited before the war by the Suffragettes, and more recently by Gandhi's followers in India, to draw attention to the plight of the unemployed. One hundred unemployed moved right into *Vogue*'s territory when they invaded the Ritz one afternoon and asked for tea, provoking press features contrasting the lives of the unemployed with those of the Ritz tea-drinkers. Another stunt took place just before Christmas, when Oxford Street was crammed with shoppers. Unemployed men lay down head to toe, eight abreast across the road, and spread over themselves posters reading 'Work or Bread'. When the police arrived and dragged them onto the pavement, they immediately went back to their places in the road and had soon created a traffic jam that paralyzed the West End.

The Hon Unity Mitford and her sister the Hon Mrs Bryan Guinness

Other facts you could not ignore were the scuffles of the Fascist party, led by Sir Oswald Mosley. Elected as Conservative member for Harrow at twenty, he had married Lord Curzon's daughter and subsequently quarrelled with both the Conservative and Labour parties. Unfortunately for him, his wife, who kept her Socialist convictions, was half Jewish. She died and left him free to marry in 1937, with Hitler as his best man, Mrs Bryan Guinness: otherwise Diana Mitford, sister of the 'Perfect Aryan Beauty' Unity Mitford. Both wives were well known to *Vogue* readers from the society pages.

For some time after Mussolini's takeover of Italy Fascism was vaguely respected, and Rothermere for the *Daily Mail* gave it his temporary support, but as the Blackshirts were seen to be using knuckledusters on hecklers and victimizing the 'Kikes' in the East End, and as Nazism grew year by year, the papers began to speak disparagingly of the 'rule of the rubber truncheon and the castor oil bottle'. In 1935 Margot Asquith was writing in *Vogue*, 'We do not believe in mock Mussolinis, silly shirts, self-advertising upstarts. We detest dictators ... Men are tired of force and formula, they ardently desire to follow the things that make for peace.' *Vogue* had mentioned Mussolini in connection with fashion in 1933: 'A propos of an article in the *Popolo d'Italia* ... Mussolini gives some good advice to the Nazis, including the warning, in view of a Prussian ordinance against lipstick and rouge - "Any power whatsoever is destined to fail before fashion. If fashion says skirts are to be short, you will not succeed in lengthening them, even with the guillotine." This statement by one dictator to another, acknowledging a power before which both are helpless, is of peculiar interest.'

Writers were now known for their politics, not their amusing novels. Evelyn Waugh was in favour of Fascism. Stephen Spender and Cecil Day Lewis represented the Left, and in spite of the Nazi hatred of modern art, Wyndham Lewis wrote a book in praise of Hitler. George Orwell, who was wounded in the Spanish Civil War, came back to write *Homage to Catalonia*; George Barker wrote his account. Aldous Huxley was now the intellectual leader of Constructive Pacifism and had published the *Encyclopedia of Pacifism*, before leaving for America with a handful of leading writers who could see the war coming and had no wish to take part in it.

In *Vogue*, the scope of the society and gossip pages was extended to include political topics. Our Lives from Day to Day took on a political flavour from the beginning of the decade. 'At Mr Wells' we began with vodka and caviare to welcome Julian Huxley back from Moscow, who spoke of communal life to as perfect a small company of famous individualists as could be gathered together in a London flat.' In the same column, an irreverent mention of Gandhi on his visit to London - 'the famous little figure ... looking very Mickey Mouse as he accepted tributes from the Ladies of India'. Asked whether he thought a dhoti sufficient garb for meeting the King, Gandhi had replied, 'The King wore enough for both of us.' On the advertising pages, readers were besought to 'Buy British', and on the fashion pages the models struck militaristic attitudes, the regimental suits that appeared in the mid-thirties giving copywriters a field day. 'Vive le Front Plisse Populaire!' ... 'Newshirts for all parties' ... 'Aux armes, Citoyennes! - the fashion cry of the moment'. Readers were told to 'March to the sound of drums by day', and shown suits with square epauletted shoulders, drummer boy frogging, gauntlet gloves and low heels, and hats with a 'forward putsch'.

One of *Vogue*'s most relevant pre-war features was a piece by Alan Stewart on finding out the real news. The silence that preceded the Abdication had

brought it home to the public that the papers did not always print the whole news. Apart from what the press overlooked and chose to suppress, there were misrepresentations and actual censorship. The press continually referred to the unemployed as if they were too idle to look for work, and to the dole as though it were a comfortable wage. The facts were finally brought home by photographs of real life cases in *Picture Post*, founded on the lines of *Life* in l938, which showed, for instance, the wife and four children of Alfred Smith waiting outside the Labour Exchange for his £2 7s. 6d. weekly dole. Most people were in the dark about Germany's new rearmed power and the fresh European threats - just before the war angry letters to *The Times* denounced the BBC for being alarmist because of its purely factual bulletins on the European situation. Alan Stewart's feature was called Every

Woman her own Tabouis - Geneviève Tabouis of the anti-Fascist *L'Œuvre* had a reputation for knowing what was going on behind the scenes. He said, 'If you lived in the United States, where the press is refreshingly bold and free, you wouldn't have to buy so many papers; but even in England you can discover almost all the news there is ... those who skim five dailies know much more than those who read one only. If you take *The Times*, you should also take the *Daily Worker*. The *Daily Telegraph* and the *News Chronicle* also balance one another nicely ... Unless you are Unity Mitford, it's unlikely that you will have much chance of a heart-to-heart talk with one of these Fuehrers, but it might be a good idea to have a look at the big shots of domestic politics. Go to a few political meetings, a Left Book Club Rally and persuade someone to get you into the House for a full dress Foreign Affairs debate.'

W H Auden in 1935, 'working on a film for the General Post Office'

IF politics were reflected only indirectly, the big scandal of the thirties happened well within *Vogue*'s scope. Mrs Simpson's name first appears in *Vogue* in 1935, obliquely mentioned in conjunction with groups including the Prince of Wales. We read that for cocktails 'hot sausages ... are out of date, back numbers. You must think up something different. The Prince of Wales has hot buttered American soda biscuits, with cod's roe, served in hot silver breakfast dishes' and, a sentence or two further down the

The Duchess of Windsor, by the end of the thirties the most unpopular woman in Britain. Cecil Beaton photographed her exclusively for *Vogue* at the Château de Candé, opposite, where she was married on 3 June 1937

example, have Schiaparelli's "pouch" dress in silk or printed cotton' - and she was photographed for *Vogue* in Schiaparelli's white linen trouser suit. When the King died, *Vogue* came out with a blank purple cover and wrote, 'The Reign Begins ... Everything we know about the new occupant of the Throne suggests a keen, alert mind and forms the image of one who has mixed with a larger number of representative men and women than most other figures in history', and in the next issue, 'Mrs Ernest Simpson is now the best dressed woman in town.' Her immaculate, pin-neat elegance, like that of another hard-edged American contemporary, Mrs Diana Vreeland, future editor of American *Vogue*, was much admired and copied in the thirties. It was a foil first for Schiaparelli's clothes, and later Mainbocher's.

Lady Furness, one of the Morgan twins who were often in *Vogue*, had introduced Mrs Simpson to the Prince of Wales and had lent her the train and feathers for the court appearance she made in spite of the rules about divorcees. In a conversation recorded by James Laver in his anthology *Between the Wars*, when Lady Furness was leaving for a few weeks' holiday, Mrs Simpson said to her, 'Oh Thelma, the little man is going to be so lonely.' 'Well, dear,' replied Lady Furness, 'You look after him while I'm away. See that he does not get into any mischief.' On her return, she and the Simpsons were guests at Fort Belvedere: 'At dinner, I noticed that the Prince and Wallis seemed to have little private jokes. Once he picked up a piece of salad with his fingers. Wallis playfully slapped his hand. I ... caught her eye and shook my head at her. She knew as well as everybody else that the Prince could be very friendly, but no matter how friendly, he never permitted familiarity ... Wallis looked straight at me. That one cold, defiant stare told me the whole story. I left the Fort the following morning.' *Vogue* published honeymoon photographs of the Duke and Duchess at Schloss Wasserleonburg, one of sixty castles put at their disposal after the Abdication, and, tremendous scoop, published a portfolio of exclusive photographs by Cecil Beaton taken of them at the Château de Candé, the Duchess in the most elegant dresses from her Mainbocher trousseau.

page, 'Mrs Simpson's food is of such a high standard that the intelligent guest fasts before going to have cocktails with her ... Hot dishes are famous.' At about this time Sir Samuel Hoare noticed Wallis Simpson for her 'sparkling jewels in very up-to-date Cartier settings'. *Vogue*'s references are so discreet that an inattentive reader might miss the point, but the two names are never far apart. 'The Prince of Wales went by boat to dine at St Tropez ... and acquired a blue and white striped sailor's pullover ... Tonight he dined at the restaurant on the quai, and when he got up to go on to another café for coffee, the entire company dining there got up and followed him, not even waiting to pay their bills ...' and in the next column, 'All the smart clothes here come from Paris and London, not St Tropez. The best-dressed women, like Mrs Ernest Simpson, for

HAD fashion been the luxury many thought it was, instead of a kind of barometer, the slump might have killed the couture - at least, for the years between the Crash and recovery. As it happened, the only Paris casualty was Augustabernard, who had just reopened in lavish new premises and who relied on a South American clientele who were all hit by the crisis at the same moment. Those houses which did not already have ready-to-wear sidelines now opened them, and even Chanel, who had one of the most expensive salons, cut her prices by half in 1932. In the first season after the Wall Street Crash, not a single American buyer came to Paris, and most of them did not return until 1933. The couture had always been prepared to wait a long time for payment, but at a time of fluctuating exchange rates this was a dangerous habit. Fortunately, all the couturiers had made so much money in the twenties that they had reserves. Their staff, who were underpaid anyway, were prepared to go on half-time, and, most important of all for the designers, the French fabric manufacturers were prepared to

supply their materials on credit. A day dress took five yards of fabric in 1938, as opposed to the two yards it would have taken in the twenties. Not surprisingly, there was a vogue for economical and washable fabrics. Chanel was invited to England by Ferguson to help promote their cottons as fashion fabrics, and in her 1931 collection she included thirty-five cotton evening dresses in piqué, lace, spotted muslin, organdie, lawn and net. These young and fresh looking dresses with their billowing skirts were the most popular evening dresses of the year with English debutantes, and with their fathers who paid the bills. Couture prices in the thirties however were not, even relatively, so very high: a plain Vionnet day dress in 1938 cost about £19, and now that it was in bad taste to look rich, there was a fashion for the 'poor' simple look. Ladies who were still fabulously rich went about in plain black dresses, furless wool coats and sweaters and slacks. *Vogue* wrote, 'It's no longer chic to be smart.' In the twenties Paris couturiers were showing 400 outfits in a single collection. In the thirties these were whittled down to a hundred, and the showings were much better organized, with bureaux for the registration of models, a black book of cheap

copyists to keep out, and press handouts to prevent misrepresentation.

It was an ill wind that made Paris less accessible to foreign clients. Now that fewer Londoners were going to Paris, London designers were given a boost and responded with new talent. Digby Morton set up his own couture business and was succeeded at Lachasse by Hardy Amies, Hartnell was prospering as the Queen's dressmaker, Molyneux and Charles Creed were to leave Paris for London at the outbreak of war. The designer Charles James, who made his reputation in America, was working in England during the early thirties and making a name for himself with the skill of his cutting and draping.

Fabrics were keeping pace with the ready-to-wear market. Artificial silk was now stronger and better made, and in 1939 the Americans began production of nylon, which they claimed to be more elastic than silk and one-and-a-half times stronger. *Vogue* drew a clothesline full of washable new clothes including a tailored linen suit, a beach dress with satinized stripes, an artificial silk jersey dress of awning stripes, and a frilled organdie and lace blouse. In shops people were asking for uncrushable fabrics like zingale, and for cottons, linens and spun rayons which were Sanforized - preshrunk. Schiaparelli matched Chanel's cottons with her own inevitably sensational experiments with Rhodophane, a glass fabric by Colcombet, and by using the nursery fabric Viyella for tailored blouses. She pioneered the use of Lightning Fasteners - zips - used first in sports skirts and finally in evening dresses, and loved to incorporate gadget clasps and motif buttons, made for her by craftsmen like Jean Clement.

The thirties in fashion was chiefly a neck and neck race between the rivals Schiaparelli and Chanel. Schiaparelli, although her influence was limited to this single decade, was the more sensational: she dressed Salvador Dali's wife free in return for inspiration, and her fashion follies were inspired jokes - the shoe hat, the 'chest of drawers' suit, the aspirin necklace and edible cinnamon buttons, the lacquered white hair. Her lasting innovation was perfectly sober - the combination of a dress with a matching jacket - but her colours were fantastic. She would put together fuchsia purple, shocking pink and black. It was typical of Schiaparelli that, when she decided she hated the modernistic mannikins given her to dress for the Exposition Internationale des Arts et Techniques in 1937, she buried them in flowers and slung up her new collection on a clothesline.

Chanel contemptuously referred to Schiaparelli as 'that Italian artist who makes clothes' (in much the same spirit as Vionnet referred to Chanel as 'that modiste'), and her own clothes of the thirties were faultlessly elegant, modern, and matchlessly chic. With Chanel No. 5 and her incredible

costume jewellery - 'It does not matter if they are real,' she said, 'so long as they look like junk!' - she revolutionized Hollywood glamour by dressing Ina Claire in the simplest of white satin pyjamas or tweed suits. Unlike Schiaparelli's musical comedy military suits, Chanel's were quite effortless, the collars small, the shoulders not noticeably padded, the waist left in its natural place. Over forty herself, she knew what made a woman look younger, and invented cardigan jackets, dashing velveteen and ciré satin cinema suits, to be worn with flattering small hats. She made hornrimmed glasses a fashion accessory, and scotched forever Dorothy Parker's overquoted remark about girls who wear glasses. Her country clothes were a revelation to tweedy Englishwomen and she was her own best advertisement. 'Chanel,' said Lesley Blanch in 1938, 'demonstrated the fact that grey flannel trousers and a hairy wool sweater are nothing if not allied to swags of pearls, wrists clogged with barbaric bracelets and a netted coiffure top-knotted with masses of geraniums and chenille plumes.'

The eagle eye of
Coco Chanel, 1939

In the twenties only two or three couturiers stood out from the crowd because the look was universal. In the thirties each house had its own look, summed up by its most famous clients. Schiaparelli dressed Daisy Fellowes, the well-known fashion individualist. Molyneux was fortunate in dressing the beautiful and stylish Princess Marina, for whom he made the most flattering and well-behaved clothes that money could buy. Mainbocher, ex-editor of French *Vogue*, followed in the same tradition but his clothes acquired a harder image through his leading customer, the Duchess of Windsor. The two most sculptural of all fashion designers both began their Paris careers in the thirties: Alix, whose draped and folded silk jerseys already identified her by her later name, Madame Grès, and Balenciaga, who came to Paris at the beginning of the Spanish Civil War and had hardly time to be appreciated before the whole

conveying the ideal realization of the dressmaker's skill and the spirit of the times. Some of the very best fashion drawings ever done were being executed at the same time by artists including Carl Ericsson (Eric), Count René Bouet Willaumez, René Bouché and Christian Bérard, a diabetic and opium addict, a gross, shabby and much-loved figure. Raoul Dufy, Giorgio de Chirico, Pavel Tchelitchew and Salvador Dali enlivened the covers and pages of *Vogue* with their drawings and paintings.

In the thirties *Vogue* began to cater for the mass fashion market. The technical improvements in fashion illustration showed the reader and the ready-to-wear manufacturers alike what to aim for, and sometimes how to cut: at first, designers had been anxious that too accurate photography could give away their secrets. The models looked as glossy and perfect as film stars, and made women want to copy their hair and make-up. The magazine helped readers directly by a concerted effort to show how to go about dressing fashionably with a limited amount of money, breaking down the given sum for essentials and accessories, leaving a margin for a beauty treatment, and adding it up neatly at the end. There was a Bargain of the Fortnight, and The Well Spent Pound, with an actual investigation into working girls' wardrobes at the end of the thirties: 'Some of the smartest girls we know turn themselves out on about £50 a year'... 'Business girls - they don't earn much - perhaps £5 a week. They perch on stools in snack bars for lunch. They save their pennies. That they can be well dressed is a miracle of England's ready-to-wear.' Suits for 6 gns., and dresses with coats for 8½ gns., began to appear from Fenwick and Jaeger, classic coats with 'nothing to date them' from Aquascutum and Harrods, and *Vogue Patterns* were devised for everything from cotton evening dresses to knitting instructions for sweaters to go under wartime uniforms. When war was finally announced *Vogue* missed an issue and then got into wartime gear with monthly, instead of fortnightly issues, to comply with government regulations. *Vogue Beauty Book* and *Vogue House and Garden Book* were incorporated, and Pattern Double Numbers stepped up. 'Our policy is to maintain the standards of civilisation ... We dedicate our pages to the support of important industries, to the encouragement of normal activities, to the pursuit of an intelligent and useful attitude to everyday affairs - and a determined effort to bring as much cheer and charm into our present life as is possible.' The first stern moral judgements - 'It's your job to spend gallantly, dress decoratively, be groomed immaculately - in short, to be a sight for sore eyes' - and condemnations of open-toed sandals in the city and women slopping about in slacks - 'Slack, we think, is the word' - gave way to talk about National Service work, blackouts, all-night canteens and cocktail-bar shelters, with an ever-increasing emphasis on practical inexpensive fashion. 'Brisk Action on the Mayfair Front' was a communiqué on the war activities of the designers - Stiebel was now a river policeman, Hardy Amies in the fire brigade, Dennis Glenny in the army, and most houses were opening up mail order departments or sending fitters out to tour the country.

Schiaparelli, above, in tweed and ermine, and, opposite, her Egyptian evening dresses of 1936

Overleaf: Christian Bérard draws. Left, Mainbocher, 1936, and right, Lelong, 1939

of Europe was at war again. Vionnet dressed Madame Martinez de Hoz, and Marcel Rochas, who is given the credit for the first padded shoulders, became famous overnight when eight ladies at a party in 1930 came face to face wearing the same Rochas dress. Charles Creed set a new standard in tailored suits for women.

By the thirties, *Vogue* had come into its fullest power over fashion. A word could make or break a collection. Couturiers would count the number of illustrations given to each house, and write off furious letters of complaint. Once the couture had recovered from the effects of the slump, it began to assume greater and greater importance. 'Now fashion is news, fashion is big business, fashion is the intimate concern of millions,' said *Vogue*, announcing in 1938 the first ever Collections Report to be broadcast from Paris to New York and relayed from there to London almost while the clothes were still being shown. A great deal of *Vogue*'s prestige was due to the metamorphosis of photography and the talents of *Vogue*'s excellent photographers. In the hands of Steichen, Hoyningen-Huene, Horst, Man Ray and Cecil Beaton, fashion photography was real art at last, technically perfect and beautifully lit,

THE first Surrealist Exhibition in England was shown in 1936, ten years after the Manifesto. It was greeted with derision. J. B. Priestley gave the reactionary view of the Surrealists when he wrote, 'They stand for violence and neurotic unreason. They are truly decadent. You catch a glimpse behind them of the deepening twilight of barbarism that may soon blot out the sky, until at last humanity finds itself in another long night ... There are about too many effeminate or epicene young men, lisping and undulating. Too many young women without manners, balance, dignity ... Too many people steadily lapsing into shaved and powdered barbarism.' Surrealism was already a familiar thing to most fashion photographers who travelled between London and Paris to work, but the exhibition made it topical and for a few years fashion illustration was dominated by Surrealism - ladies in evening dress carrying their own heads, models coiled in rope or poised by cracked mirrors, others sitting in evening dress with brooms and buckets, or on rubbish heaps. Dr M. F. Agha, Art Editor-in-Chief of *Vogue*, felt it necessary to write an explanatory dialogue: 'No one can tell me exactly what a Surrealist is. Can you?' 'A Surrealist is a man

who likes to dress like a fencer, but does not fence; to wear a diving-suit, but does not dive ... but descends to the lower depths of the subconscious ... You know the old formula: "Man Bites Dog"? - only in this case the Dog has Paranoia, and the Man is really a couple of other guys.'

In a Surrealist film you could see, among other things, a cow sleeping in a Louis XIV salon; a man kicking a blind beggar; a burning tree, a giraffe, and a plough being thrown out of a window. At the end of the first performance of this, the producers were beaten up by the audience. Salvador Dali, below, who received reporters sitting on top of a desk on top of a bed with a loaf of bread on his head, drew for *Vogue* his Dream House designs for the New York World's Fair in 1939. *Vogue* wrote, 'three live mermaids ... swim through flexible, rubberoid branches of trees, past long tendrils of typewriters. They swim past a writhing woman, chained to a piano, with the piano keys carved out of her rubberoid stomach ... On a mammoth bed, a live woman is lying, asleep and dreaming three dreams ... a double row of grisly, make-believe women, crowned with lobsters and girdled with eels, fades away into the distance.'

Jean Cocteau brings his drawings to London in 1936

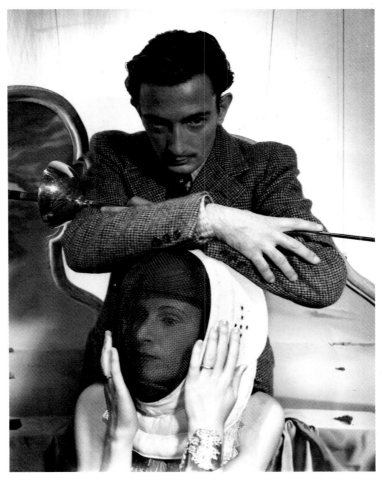

Rodgers and Hart's musical parody of Dali, opposite, and the real thing,
above, Dali's costumes for the ballet Bacchanale

IN direct opposition to the effects of the slump on pre-war fashion, there was the irresistible, saturating glamour of American films. If the rich looked to Paris for their new fashions, working girls and the couturiers themselves kept an eye on the movies, 'the most perfect visual medium for the exploitation of fashion and beauty that ever existed'. Formerly the most vulgar dresses and hats

Joan Crawford, above, in Schiaparelli, 1932, and the young Vivien Leigh, opposite, in Victor Stiebel, 1936, a couple of years before Gone with the Wind

of the early Gloria Swanson type, seen at fashion shows, provoked whispers among *Vogue*'s editor of 'Phew! Pretty Hollywood!' but around the late twenties films caught up with fashion. One of the first attempts to reconcile film costume with real life fashion came in 1929, when Chanel was invited to Hollywood. It was a miserable failure. Elegant, contemporary and revolutionary though they were

when Chanel designed them, the clothes dated overnight when hems dropped, and films still 'in the can' were suddenly obsolete. Nevertheless, the revolution went on. Stars of great personal chic refused to be dressed like Christmas trees in films, and 'bright young playwrights pointed out that duchesses do not eat breakfast in ballgowns,' as Lesley Blanch wrote. Schiaparelli, Marcel Rochas, Molyneux, Alix, Jean Patou and Lanvin all made the trip to Hollywood, but this expensive and clumsy business gradually gave way to reliance on Hollywood's own indigenous and talented designers, the best-known of whom were Adrian and Howard Greer. By 1933 the question 'Who did that look first, Hollywood or Paris?' was inextricable, and *Vogue*, seriously attempting to work it out in a feature called Does Hollywood Create?, came to the conclusion that fashion ideas arrive 'by a sort of spontaneous combustion', giving credit for the fashion for pageboy hair to Garbo, feather boas to Marlene Dietrich, and accolades for a sixth sense about the fashion future to Adrian and Howard Greer, who had to design their costumes months ahead of the release date, and make clothes that would not look outdated at the end of the run, perhaps two years later.

James Laver in *Vogue* called the camera the first 'engine for imposing types of beauty' and pointed out that 'one curious result of the power of the film has been the spread of type-consciousness to classes which have previously known nothing of such conceptions'. Every important film star appeared in *Vogue* and contributed some new look or fashion:

Garbo - hollowed eye sockets and plucked eyebrows
Dietrich - plucked eyebrows and sucked-in cheeks
Joan Crawford - the bow-tie mouth
Tallulah Bankhead - a sullen expression
Mae West - the hourglass figure and an
*   attractive bawdiness*
Constance Bennett - a glazed, bandbox smartness
Jean Harlow - platinum hair
Katherine Hepburn - red curls and freckles
Vivien Leigh - gypsy colouring, a glittering combination
*   of white skin, green eyes and dark red hair*

Vogue's models were often recognizable copies of these types of beauty, and in the thirties they were photographed in cinematographic style: in statuesque bias-cut white satin evening dresses draped on sofas beside glass bowls of white tulips, and lit from one side. It was a symptom of the new acceptability of films that *Vogue* took sittings on location out to Elstree studios, and photographed behind the scenes during filming, showing such oddities as a row of girls waiting to go on in Wanger's film *Vogues of 1938* resting their arms in arm stalls, 'necessary precaution against the least wrinkle, the slightest crease'.

Single-handed, Hollywood evolved make-up from the crude materials of the twenties into the gigantic industry it is today. In 1931 the *Sunday Express* calculated that 1,500 lipsticks were being sold in London shops for every one sold ten years previously. Cosmetics and nail enamel were now sold from all hairdressers, large stores, chemists and Woolworths, and were applied with a skill learnt from the screen and from magazines. 'Glamour is all,' said *Vogue* in 1935, and tried to pin down what it meant: 'We decided it was the quality of illusion, not just personality. After all, Hitler has personality, but you couldn't call him glamorous.' When Adrian wrote about dressing Garbo for *Camille* he said, 'She brought to the sets, with her quality of aloofness, that mystery which is a part of her and a part of the theatre's integral glamour.' Unattainable glamour, embodied in the most famous stars of the thirties, Garbo and Dietrich, was the wistful other side of the threadbare thirties.

Make-up features in *Vogue* in the twenties had been rare and tentative, but in the thirties readers were taught the techniques of the stars, point by point. In Seven Steps to Stardom, a beauty feature in January 1938, an ordinary looking girl is transformed into a Glamour Girl: first, a found-ation of greasepaint over the face, with a streak of darker greasepaint narrowing the jaw, then blended eye shadows hollowing the eyes. Eyebrow pencil fines the browline, powder and rouge are brushed on and off again with a soft brush, lashes are blackened with mascara and thickened with artificial eyelashes. Finally, the mouth is defined with a pencil line and filled in with lipstick or lip rouge. In this way, glamour was thoroughly analyzed and its effects calculated. When *Vogue* asked George Gershwin what he noticed first about a woman, he gave an answer typical of the new attitude:

At 40 paces - her shape
At 25 paces - her ankles and shoes
At 10 paces - her face
At 8 paces - her eyes
At 5 paces - her mouth
At no paces - her conversation.

Imported together with Hollywood innovations like false fingernails and eyelashes - which had to be applied separately with glue - there was the new slang, assimilated just as readily. *Vogue* first used the adjective 'sexy' to describe an evening dress in 1936, the year of Lesley Blanch's first article as features editor of *Vogue*. Called 'On dit - and how!', it incorporated the new American expressions and described the new tone of voice. 'Mayfair is quite "sold" on American slang, and you have only to

enter any one of these drawing rooms to be engulfed in a spate of transatlanticisms, which describe "swell guys" as being "the tops" or, its equivalent, "the Camembert"; "swell gals" as being "pretty smooth"; any variety of pleasures as "easy to take"; while the finer shades of pathos and bathos are now familiar to us as "sob-stuff" or "the jerkers". "Am I right, or am I *right*?" as they would phrase it.'

Hollywood films of the thirties followed the pattern of the Depression and the New Deal. The first years of the Depression brought in Frankenstein and Dracula, followed by the realistic gangster film, Hollywood's attempt to attract an increasingly critical audience. Based on headline news stories, these ran straight into opposition from legions and

clubs like the Daughters of the American Revolution, who objected that villains like Edward G. Robinson in *Little Caesar* had been turned into heroes, and who took offence at Spencer Tracy's words in *Quick Millions*: 'I'm too nervous to steal, too lazy to work ... a man's a fool to go into legitimate business when you can clean up by applying business methods to organizing crime.' The 'confession' film, about girls who had traded on sex in the past and were trying to live it down, was almost as objectionable to moral America. In the purge that followed, film companies fell over backwards to comply with the Hays Office new Production Code. Jean Harlow's new film *Born to be Kissed* was changed in a moment of panic to *100 Per Cent Pure*, then more soberly renamed *The Girl from Missouri*. Hollywood then turned with relief to a sweeter and safer day. Films based on Dickens, Louisa May Alcott and Barrie brought to the screen Victorian life seen through a mist of nostalgia. The New Deal also brought in family films, musical spectaculars and screwball comedies.

The spread of type-consciousness: Katherine Hepburn, opposite, the thinking woman's comedienne; a windblown Hedy Lamarr, above left; and a polished Loretta Young, above right

Neo-Victorianism was a major influence in the thirties. Victorian revivals like Dumas's *Lady of the Camellias* and Wilde's *The Importance of Being Earnest* were very popular on the stage, and so were modern plays on Victorian subjects like *The Barretts of Wimpole Street*: at one moment, three pseudo-historical plays about the Brontës were running at the same time.

The most successful of all musical, historical and costume shows was C. B. Cochran's 1932 production of Noël Coward's *Cavalcade*, a variety show that evoked the patriotism, security and sentiments of the Victorian age, and which appeared just when a great national effort was being made to overcome the Depression. A cast of 400 was brought up to the stage by six hydraulic lifts. *Vogue* wrote, 'Coming late into the darkened theatre, I was thrust into a world of 1900 ... one of the actors stepped out in front of the curtain and announced the thrilling news that Mafeking had been relieved ... the next scene revealed, not the stage, but the audience - a theatre of 1900 going mad over a Boer War victory; the people jumping from box to box, embracing one another; the women throwing fans into the air; the men their coats, ties and hats. The enthusiasm was infectious, and the whole theatre went mad, some people bursting into hysterical sobbing.' Coward said himself at the first night, 'In spite of the troublous times we are living in, it is still a pretty exciting thing to be English.' The British cinema also scored a major success with a historical subject, Alexander Korda's *The Private Life of Henry VIII* with Charles Laughton, followed by *Catherine the Great* with Flora Robson. There was a vogue for slashed and padded sleeves, velvet Tudor halos, shallow boaters with ribbon streamers as worn by Katherine Hepburn in *Little Women*, leg-of-mutton sleeves, and, from Norma Shearer in the film version of *Romeo and Juliet*, the Juliet bob, the Juliet cap, and the long, demure frock of full-skirted velvet with touches of white. The Victorian revival did not stop at clothes: in odd conjunction with functionalism, people were buying Victorian knick-knacks, sprigged curtains and heavy patterned wallpapers.

The movement was reinforced by Queen Elizabeth's own personal taste. With a good old-fashioned Scottish upbringing, she had conservative tastes and a love of daring finery. Dressed by Norman Hartnell, she wore velvet or furred suits, jewellery, flowers in the morning, a picture hat and a long full dress for receptions, and a crinoline for evening - 'full-skirted and decolleté in the Victorian, off-the-shoulder manner', and often in her favourite colour, powder blue. *Vogue* said, 'She is not a "fashionable" woman in the usual sense of the word. Yet her clothes superbly fulfil the two fundamental canons of good dressing. They fit her personality like a glove; and they are brilliantly suited to her way of life.' Her clothes on tour were tremendously admired and enjoyed by the public in France, America and Canada. In 1937 and 1938 every designer had fallen for the fairytale glamour of the sentimental crinoline - Patou, Molyneux, even Chanel, Vionnet and Alix.

The Duchess of Kent, Princess Marina, had lived with her father in Paris, and her sophisticated and innate elegance were Molyneux's best advertisement. *Vogue* drew a comparison between the Duchess and her great-aunt Queen Alexandra: 'There is the same classic purity of line, the same air of aloof elegance: the same charming, vague, rather wry smile: the same coiffure is topped by an identical hat ... Women scan the papers for the Duchess's confirmation of fashion's newest trends.'

Lanvin's 'State Banquet' dress with Victorian jewellery, 1938, opposite. The Duchess of York, below, with the Princess Elizabeth, 1930

THE health movement of the thirties made holiday camps popular, country resorts where campers lived in wooden huts and had their meals provided for them, spending their time walking, sunbathing, playing games and singing around the camp fire. *Vogue* went on location to take photographs round the floodlit Roehampton swimming club, showed playsuits and swimsuits in every summer issue, and advertised the new John Lewis country club, only thirty-five minutes from Paddington, where members could play tennis and croquet, go punting or swimming, and attend concerts and dances in the evening: 'The total bill for a weekend from Saturday afternoon to Sunday evening need not be more than ten shillings.' Sunbathing, nudism and hiking had all come from Germany at the time of the Weimar Republic, and all through the thirties Austria and Germany were the fashionable places for holidays abroad. Even in August 1939 *Vogue* included an advertisement for the German Railways Information Bureau: 'Germany, Land of Hospitality, offers everything you could wish for your holiday'. The result in fashion was a craze for Tyrolean peasant costume. The *Wandervogel* with his *lederhosen* was the romantic extension of the British hiker with his open-neck shirt, Borotra beret and shorts, and women took to dirndls of bright cheap cotton with a tight bodice, a bib or daisy braces, an apron and a feathered hat. 'The English have adopted the Tyrol as their own,' said *Vogue*, and described the same state of affairs in Paris, where the Princesse de Faucigny-Lucinge (Baba d'Erlanger that was) had just opened a shop selling only Tyrolean beachwear.

Open-air living had made women body-conscious and health-conscious. The slimming crazes of the twenties continued, but with the emphasis on keeping fit. Mrs Syrie Maugham, the decorator, was an obsessive dieter. 'Monday. Went to the first of Mrs Maugham's diet lunch parties ... She decided to devote the first quiet spell to the interests of health and made it known to her friends that any who were feeling the effects of overeating and such a long siege of strenuous partying could come any day to lunch or dine with her on regime food.' Mrs Maugham finally went on the diet of diets. 'I starved for six weeks. Yes, literally, for six weeks I ate nothing at all ... yet I never missed a day's work and feel better than I can ever remember.'

Vogue profiled a New York model school in 1938, forerunner of those we know today, with 'Buddha' exercises, book-balancing for poise, lessons in dancing and make-up. People were so geared to keeping fit that the slightest excuse was enough to begin a craze for some particular exercise: when there was a French taxi strike in spring 1936, *Vogue* found 'Tout Paris on Wheels', men in dinner suits bicycling to the opera and women getting special cycling suits made up - Princesse de Faucigny-Lucinge rode tandem in a grey flannel shorts suit. The craze spread to the country, where country house stables were being filled up with secondhand bicycles for weekend guests. For those in London who would rather lose a few inches lying prone, Elizabeth Arden devised a warm paraffin Pack Treatment. The most popular way to get thin and healthy in the thirties was by dancing, and *Vogue* recommended tap lessons with Bunny Bradley, 'where Mr Cochran sends all his Young Ladies to be finished', and ballet with Marie Rambert - together with a caution about taking it too seriously if you were already in your twenties. Zelda Fitzgerald's efforts to reach a professional standard when she was long past the ballet beginner age had contributed to her breakdown.

VOGUE

DOUBLE NUMBER 1/6
with VOGUE PATTERN BOOK
including Clothes for the North
JULY · 20 · 1932 (15)
The Condé Nast Publications Ltd.

In 1936 Wilder Hobson wrote in *Vogue*, 'Swing is the musical fashion of the hour. Not to know the work of such swing artists as Thomas 'Fats' Waller and Jack 'Big Gate' Teagarden (gate meaning the ability to swing) is to confess such a dowdiness as would have been shown some years ago by someone who supposed the rumba to be one of the larger vertebrae. Judging by the heavy white-tie and Schiaparelli attendance at such New York swing saloons as the Onyx Club, swing music has penetrated the ritziest circles. It is even robust enough to appeal to Ernest Hemingway.' On liners, in the new Dorchester and the Savoy, down at the Locarno in Streatham, or even at home with the radiogram, people dressed up to the nines and danced all night to the smooth, glamorous sound of the big bands with their ranks of trumpets, clarinets and drums. The big bands, like some of the big cinemas, included crooners, tap dancers and showgirls in their performances, and teams of virtuosi would get to their feet and take the lead, playing extempore. Idols of the cinema audiences and best-loved of all the dancers in the dancing thirties - apart from the dazzling teenage Margot Fonteyn - were Fred Astaire and Ginger Rogers, one of whose most popular films was *The Castles*, about the earlier dancers Vernon and Irene Castle, *Vogue*'s heroine of the magazine's first decade. But whoever you were, you had to have rhythm. In the words of Irving Berlin's song, played by Jimmie Lunceford's band in 1937,

He ain't got rhythm
Every night he sits in the house alone.
'Cos he ain't got rhythm
Every night he sits there and wears a frown.
He attracted some attention
When he found the fourth dimension,
But he ain't got rhythm
So no one's with him
The loneliest man in town ...

Louis Armstrong and Duke Ellington came on tour to show how swing should be played, and all the new dances came over from America. In February 1938 a forerunner of jitterbugging arrived in London, called 'The Big Apple', opposite, a black euphemism for bottom. It involved lots of steps, including 'Kickin' the Mule', 'Truckin' and 'Peelin' the Apple'. Lesley Blanch, writing about it in *Vogue*, came to the sad conclusion that the British did not have rhythm. 'Nostalgic university dons and their wives, in white tennis shoes and cross garters hung with little bells, bouncing dankly through the naiveties of *Parson's Wedding* and *Jenny Pluck Pears*, cannot be considered to represent the dancing public ... (They) go to the Hammersmith Palais de Dance, the Astoria in the Charing Cross Road, the new Paramount in Tottenham Court Road ... to dance to first class bands of the Henry Hall and Roy Fox Kidney, for 1*s.* 6*d.* in the afternoon and 2*s.* 6*d.* in the evening ... the Big Apple demands a complete unselfconsciousness, which is not our national forte.'

THE thirties changed the style of living and entertaining. People with town houses who had kept two or three servants now had only a cook. They closed up their basements, used the breakfast room as a kitchen, added a bath on the first floor and lived more or less as if they were in a flat. Cocktail parties turned into snack dinners. 'One has a sandwich, a whisky-and-soda, and goes in for a good supper after the play. I wonder if dinner is disappearing from our social scheme of life?' wondered *Vogue* in 1932. A few years later, even grand dinner parties turned out simpler food. 'Nobody has grand food any more ... at Lady Colefax, we ate macaroni with cream and cheese, lamb with mint sauce, potato croquettes and spinach, and apple charlotte.' House decoration was simplified and functional. Reinforced concrete staircases corkscrewed up to the ceiling, opposite, and lighting was much improved by indirect lights. Opaque bowls were set directly into the ceiling or walls, and the 'Anglepoise' reading lamps were introduced. The photographer Hoyningen-Huene mentioned the importance of good lighting when he was asked about the new Brick Top premises he had been asked to decorate in Paris: 'I am going to light up the cabaret so that, after midnight, it will be becoming to middle-aged people who are slightly under the influence of liquor.' Schiaparelli's London flat was furnished entirely from John Lewis, below. 'It is so smart, so right and so practical' - with unpainted wood tables, rush-seat stools and armchair and divan covered in an unpatterned glazed chintz at 2s. 11d. a yard. Chanel's house at Cap Martin, left, was also the 'essence of simplicity, without superfluous furniture. But what there is is the most perfect of its kind: old oak tables, chests, and cupboards, and in the airy bedrooms old Italian beds.'

*Frederick Ashton by
Cecil Beaton*

*Lady Abdy dressed as a
Siamese dancer,
attended by a semi-nude
slave, at the Colonial
Ball in Paris, 1931*

SOME of the best parties were described by Cecil Beaton in his Social Scene column. There were mystery parties like the one at which the footmen carried in a trunk, and everyone was asked to guess who was inside. The trunk was opened and a lady stepped out in a mask, scarf, heavy gloves and high boots. Mrs Michael Arlen guessed right: it was Gaby Morlay, the French actress. There were musical parties, like the one where Serge Lifar kicked off his shoes, leapt onto the piano and performed an impromptu dance. There was a craze for Victorian games like musical chairs, blindman's buff, and bobbing for apples - in 1932 'the latter game went out of favour very quickly as none of the women would risk losing their new eyelashes'. Most popular and exciting of all were the Scavenger parties started by Mrs Marshall Field in London and immediately copied by Elsa Maxwell. Dinner guests were given a list of things to obtain, and the one who collected most between ten and midnight won. Here is Elsa Maxwell's list:

> *One red bicycle lamp*
> *One cooked sausage*
> *One live animal other than a dog*
> *One swan from the Bois de Boulogne*
> *One slipper worn by Mistinguette that night*
> *One handkerchief belonging to the
>   Baron Maurice de Rothschild*
> *One hat from Mrs Reginald Fellowes*
> *One live Duchess*
> *One autographed photograph of royalty signed that night*
> *One Metro ticket*
> *One mauve comb*
> *Three red hairs*
> *One pompom from a sailor's hat*
> *The cleverest man in Paris*

That night, Mistinguette came offstage to find her dressing room ransacked and all her shoes gone.

The next day, they were returned tied to flowering trees and bunches of white orchids.

Elsa Maxwell gave *Vogue* her seven rules for a good party. Ruthlessness - no lame ducks, no churchmen, no financiers or diplomats. Never let guests do what they want - guests never want to do what they want. Cram them into one room, which should be too small for the number invited. Light that room brilliantly. Never show any anxiety. Try to incur some opposition so that people take sides. Keep up plenty of noise. 'I once gave a party in a room too cold and cavernous ... so I hastily procured some beehives and, successfully concealing them in the room, the ears of the guests were assailed by a pleasant buzzing during lulls in the music.'

One of the wittiest parties was given by Miss Olga Lynn, at which guests were asked to come as a well-known book or play. Lady Eleanor Smith was *Vile Bodies*, Evelyn Waugh came as Wyndham Lewis's new book which was so expensive no one could afford it, Tallulah Bankhead was *The Open Book*, and Lord Knebworth, 'who sported a photograph of a Very August Pair', was *The Good Companions*.

In summer 1938 Lady Mendl gave a huge circus party, on Gatsby proportions. The hostess, in aquamarines, diamonds and a white organdie Mainbocher, was the ringmaster in the tan-bark ring, with acrobats in satin and paillettes, ponies and clowns. Guests danced on a special composition dance floor under which there were millions of tiny springs, so that it gently heaved up and down with the rhythm. Constance Spry sent three aeroplanes of roses from London to Paris for the party, and in different parts of the garden three orchestras played jazz, Cuban rumbas and Hungarian waltzes. Concealed lighting turned the garden into a dream landscape with marble statues, fountains and urns of cut flowers ...

For most of the people there, it was the last party.

By 1941 Londoners had settled down to a routine of chaos. Life was not only dangerous, but uncomfortable, dirty and odd. There were rabbits and chickens in backyards and on roofs, the park flower beds were full of cabbages and carrots, and habitual reserve gave way to smiles and offers of drinks. At the station, you were asked, 'Is your journey really necessary?' and a woman porter helped you with your cases. Places of entertainment were temporarily shut, and instead people went out to sleep; either in the dank and smelly municipal shelters or the muggy, convivial underground where, if you were lucky - or unlucky, some said - there might be an E.N.S.A. concert. People talked a different language, borrowed from the RAF, summed up by David Langdon in his cartoon of two civil servants, 'Give me a buzz on the intercom at eleven hundred hours and we'll bale out for coffee.'

Vetustisima Templariorum Porticu
Igne consumpta
Anº 1678
Nova Hæc
Sumptibus Medij Templi extructa
Anº 1681
Gulielmo Whitelocke Arm Thefaur

Round every bombed house there spread a circle of debris, broken glass and pulverized coal which gradually settled on every surface, together with the Blitz smell of charred timber, gas and watersoaked dust. In the middle of the Blitz *Vogue* wrote, '"Come in and have a bath" rather than a drink, is the new social gesture - soap and water being a far more pleasing offer than any amount of gin.' The population was continually moving about, whether bombed out, evacuating, or snatching a weekend's leave at home. The big hotels were crowded out. 'They are like luxury liners, their passengers signing on for an endlessly protracted, portless voyage.' They slept uneasily in the littered lounges, ate and danced in their crumpled clothes to the band - perhaps Lew Stone - while over their heads the roof spotters scanned the dark city. The problem of what to take with you, even for a night in the shelter, was a nightmare. 'All life is now lived in suitcases ... the luggage-lugger has to decide between staggering under her all, or travelling light and free, but risking a return to nothing but demolition squads at work in the remnants of the area. "Safe as houses" now seems an obsolete phrase, and in rather poor taste, too.'

It became common practice when you had dinner with friends to stay the night there. Guests camped in the basement or the bathroom, and dinner menus became a great deal simpler. 'You take what you can get, and make what you can of it, very often having to cook on an open fire, too. Onions being as scarce as peaches, even the most elegant cook can no longer baulk at hot-pots or stews as dinner-party fare.' *Vogue*'s social editor changed her milieu: 'A recent alarm found the Dorchester shelter filling up with celebrities - several ministers without portfolios or gas masks either, Lady Diana Cooper in full evening dress, Vic Oliver in serious mood, his wife Sarah Churchill sound asleep on the floor, and Leonora Corbett trying out a new hairdo.' When the siren sounded in Mayfair, it often as not found the couturiers in the middle of complicated fittings. Captain Molyneux, his mouth full of pins, would ask his model, 'Do you want to go to the shelter?' and Sheila Wetton, later *Vogue*'s senior fashion editor, would obediently shake her head. At John Lewis the fittings were carried on in their shelters, while Dickens and Jones provided canteen refreshments for bomb-bound customers. 'At Grosvenor House, the new deep-shelter restaurant defies even sirens. It's left to the band to play All Clear, fitting the phrase to various tunes ... Cinemas now flash All Clear! All Clear! across the screen regardless of the picture. It looked wonderful scrawled across Lillian Russell's 1880 bust, the other night.'

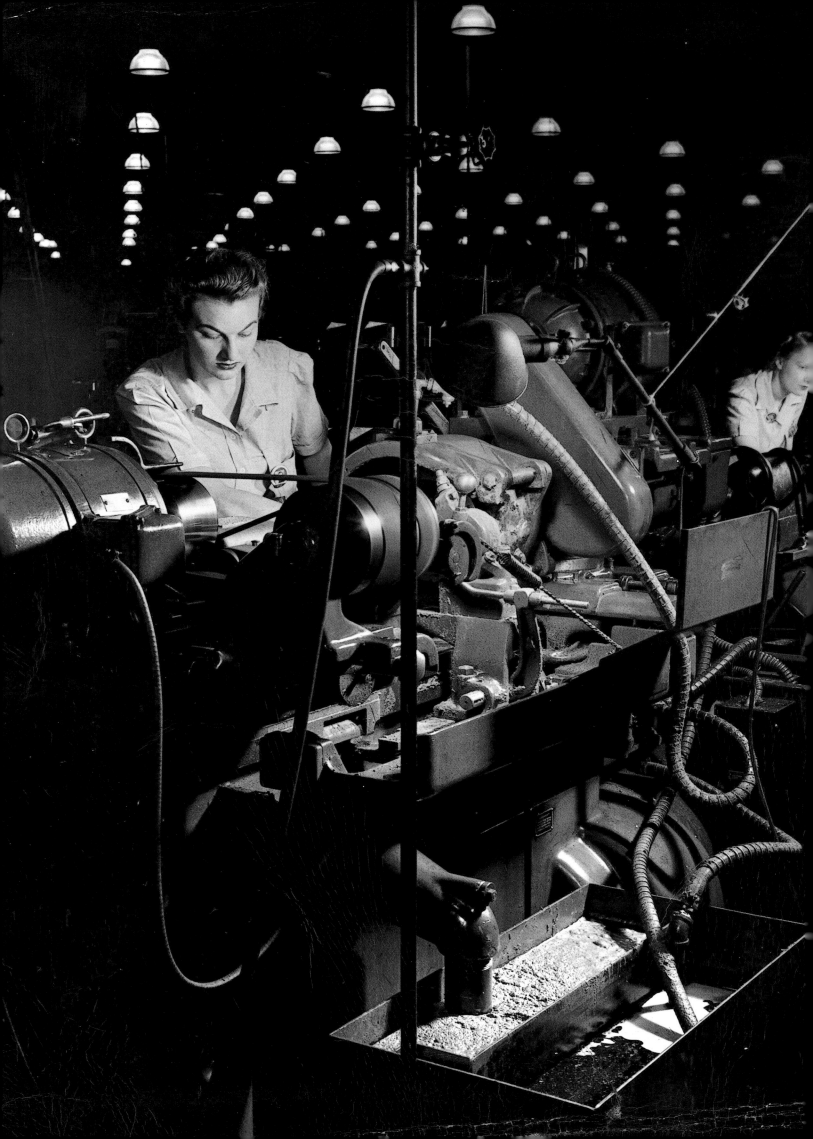

VOGUE wrote complementary features, 'I'm just back from town' and 'I'm just back from the country', giving the flavour of life in the summer of 1941. In town, 'Whole chunks of streets are up, choking dust turning people white ... powdered glass tinkling about and everyone being too, too normal ... errand girls instead of boys, bus conductorettes, waitresses at the Mirabelle ... Piccadilly pretties now strut around in pseudo-sensible slacks ... there are enormous determined cinema queues, and the Vic Wells ballet back again, and Flanagan and Allen, Oi-ing their way through the Black Vanities show, the theatrical success of the moment ... You can hire hens by the week, they lay all over the back yard or balcony ... in the evening nothing is fixed up ahead, and no one dreams of dressing up at night ... Potato Bars have taken over from Milk Bars, and restaurants are full up all the time; an endless chain of meals emerging one into the next, all overlapping, women looking extra well groomed in uniform ... Everyone's talking about Gerald Kelly's portrait of the Queen - we all know she has the most dazzling pink and white complexion, but why leave out the white? ... everywhere, the shrugging, shrilling Free French, the brightly coloured uniforms that fill the streets.' The progress of the war could be charted by the foreign uniforms in London. Together with the allied troops, nearly 1½ million overseas troops were billeted in this country during the war.

In the country, 'all the big houses are commandeered ... ambulance classes, knitting bees for the Women's Institute, dressing for dinner with rigid formality, canteen stints and voluntary shifts of tractor driving and dairy work, everyone bicycling ... the difficulty of obtaining cosmetics - home-brewed lotions in the chemist's shop, car owners taking it in turns to drive into the nearest town with huge lists to do everyone's shopping for the week ... the farmer's wife sleeps under the dairy table with both her children, the vicar's wife makes for the crypt in her siren suit, the doctor's wife shares her fully equipped Anderson shelter.'

Weddings highlighted the many little austerities and restrictions of wartime life in Britain, from the rushed proposal to the ban on rice-throwing. Church bells were only to ring in case of parachute landings, there was no choir, no sugar icing for the cake, 'so enchanting tea-cosy covers have been invented to fit over plain cakes. For flowers and food, the bride takes what she can get ... the regimental flower, badge or squadron crest carried out in colour, the bouquet a mixed nosegay of any flowers in season, since the hot-houses are occupied by fruit and vegetables.' The honeymoon might be a weekend in a borrowed cottage, petrol carefully saved for the purpose, or a few days in London, taking the opportunity of collecting your friends together 'since no knowing, these days, when the next meeting may be'. The best presents were practical, 'a portable wireless or gramophone, a portable Electrolux refrigerator that works on oil, electricity or gas ... treasures that money can't buy - a petrol coupon, honey in the comb, home-made jam'.

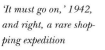

'It must go on,' 1942, and right, a rare shopping expedition

The 'Lend a hand on the land' posters brought townspeople into the country to help with the digging or haymaking. They were a mixed blessing to farmers, particularly the girls who turned up in high heels and their best dresses, but there were other more reliable sources of labour - soldiers, released from barracks for the day, and prisoners-of-war, working bands of thirty or forty Germans or

Lady Diana Cooper, opposite, boils up the swill

Italians dressed in blue dungarees patched with green. *Vogue* photographer Norman Parkinson had volunteered for the Navy but had been told, 'You'd be more useful to us as a photographer'. He now worked on a propaganda magazine repudiating the statements of Lord Haw-Haw, and ran a farm at the same time. *Vogue* sent all the clothes for their country fashion shots down on the train, and Parkinson photographed them between mucking out the pigs and collecting swill. He wrote about the farm, 'Hotels, cafés and the cinema have bins with Park's Pig Food on the lid ... we collect the bins from the back door at four, and return for dinner by the front at eight. "Leave plenty on the side of your plate," we remind each other. "More for our pigs." '

Another Londoner running a farm was Lady Diana Cooper, who had set up a productive and profitable business with three acres, a cow and £50, and managed it single-handed until she accompanied her husband to Singapore. No Marie Antoinette, this amazingly versatile and adventurous society beauty, who had toured Europe and America as an actress, got up at 6.30 to milk the cow, feed the animals and make cheese. Another linchpin of London society, Cecil Beaton, went down to photograph her, and was brainwashed. 'When you take into consideration the fact that their eggs replace "fixed" price fish, rare meat, or the canned foods which should be kept for emer-

gency, fowls cannot fail to pay their way,' he wrote with wonder and awe. 'By adding scrap to the rationed quota more fowls can be fed than have rations allotted to them.' Meanwhile Mrs John Betjeman in Berkshire was running a large vegetable and herb garden with the help of two evacuee schoolmasters, milking her goats twice a day, driving herself about in a dogcart and riding the dawn parachute patrol on the downs.

In November 1942, *Vogue* pointed out to its readers another line of war work - welcoming the American servicemen to Britain. 'Remember, everything is twice as much fun to these American boys if there's a girl in it ... Frankness and informality are the keynotes to strike ... The American gullet is used to iced whisky, iced beer ... they'll like to hear the local history and superstitions.' In the pursuit of girls, the Americans had everything their own way. They were paid at least four times the basic British pay, they drove huge flashy cars, dispensed nylons, candy and packets of Lucky Strike, and gave their girlfriends a taste of glamour at the American base dances, with lavish food and drink, and the top dance bands like Glen Miller's, here on tour. As the British serviceman bitterly remarked, 'The Americans are all right, except that they are overpaid, oversexed and over here.' When they finally departed things became a little greyer and quieter. Marghanita Laski remarked in 1946 *Vogue*, you couldn't count on finding a taxi outside the American Red Cross Clubs, and the young girls in the tube weren't chewing gum any more.

The immediate effects of the war on *Vogue* had been to put up the price from 1*s*. to 2*s*. in 1940, 2*s*. 6*d*. with *Vogue Pattern Book* included, and finally 3*s*. in 1942; and to contract the number of pages because of the paper shortage. Maxims such as 'Waste paper is vital to the war effort' and 'Use as little paper as possible for fires' were printed at the foot of the pages. The circulation, however, increased, climbing from 52,000 in 1941 to 106,000 in 1949, and each issue was passed from hand to hand until up to twenty women had seen it. *Vogue*'s own advertisement in May 1941 said, 'Many more women are now buying *Vogue* than, on an average, used to take it in pre-war days. You've a copy in your hands - you're lucky. But every month there are countless people who miss their *Vogue* ... The trouble is, of course, that owing to official restrictions in the supply of paper, we just can't print as many copies as we'd like to. So it's a question of first come, first served. Please, if you're one of these fortunate first, don't be dog-in-a-manger about your *Vogue*. Share it with your friends. Invite them home and give them the run of your copy. And then, when you've read it all, studied it all and planned all your outfits - pass it on to someone else.'

Most women found the disappearance of stockings and cosmetics even harder to accept than dress restrictions. The decline and fall of the stocking was the decline and fall of women's morale. The first blow was the ban on silk stockings in 1941, when, in January, *Vogue* recommended the substitutes - cotton, rayon and the hard-wearing heavy mesh - but by August even these were in such short supply that the

advice became 'Discard stockings for casual wear at home and in the country substituting a plausible cream make-up ... wear sturdy stockings whenever suitable ... wash and darn your precious rayons tenderly, taking them to the invisible menders at the first hint of a ladder.' Leg paint turned out to be thoroughly unsatisfactory, some kinds turning yellow in daylight, others rubbing off on skirts and leaving

Tough jobs, tough clothes, Land Girls, opposite, and an A.T.S. searchlight crew, 1943

indelible marks. Worse was to come. By 1942 the Board of Trade warned that if women didn't go without stockings during the summer they would have to by winter. In a feature called Sock Shock, *Vogue* bravely published a picture of a woman in a smart summer afternoon dress, big hat - and ankle socks. 'Socks can contrive to look charming,' said *Vogue* brazenly. 'But we believe that it's easier to achieve a smart stockingless appearance with quite bare legs (smoothly tanned or made up) and footlets. We hope the Board will put these in production,' and meanwhile offered a knitting pattern for them. Lux advertisements, reminding the reader that Lux would one day come back on the market, ran this rhyme in 1945:

No wonder Julia shouts hurray!
Her sweetheart's home on leave today,
And frequent washing in the past
Has made his favourite stockings last.

Vogue's tone of voice had changed radically in the three years between 1939, when an editorial had rapped women over the knuckles for slopping about in town wearing open-toed sandals and slacks, and 1941: 'For the A.R.P. worker, the new, short coiffure. Long hair can be tied into a net turban which will hide under a tin hat. For the face, no make-up, but a non-greasy, all-purpose cream, dusted with powder ... Save your cosmetics for evenings out ... That "too-

good-to-be-true" look which only a personal maid can produce is absent - because the maid is absent, on munitions ... Clothes look as if they had been taken care of, put on beautifully and then forgotten for more important things.' *Vogue*'s special issues were now devoted to Patterns and Renovations. At the beginning of the war, when there was still a pretence that fashion was changing and developing year by year, there were diagrams showing how you could alter last year's looks to this year's: later on, *Vogue* turned its attention to making the best of things. 'You can go hatless if you wear simple swept-back hair like this ... you can go stockingless if you wear simple flat-heeled shoes like this.' Needs must, and the beauty pages, shrinking with the shrinking supply of cosmetics, extolled the virtues of a healthy, brisk, scrubbed appearance. 'Polish yourself up: hair burnished and crisply cropped to the new length - it's a look that does not jar with uniform - with women's uniform. Somehow, more and more, the eye unconsciously measures women up by this yardstick. Why does that shoulder-mane seem so out of date? Because it would look messy hanging on a uniform collar ... What's wrong with those exquisite tapered nails? They couldn't do a hand's turn without breaking. The woman who could change instantly into uniform, or munitions overalls and look charming, soignée and right, is the smart woman of today.' Women were exhorted to keep 'nails rosy till the day when varnish vanishes: figure kept taut by exercise and good posture, with corsets a helping, but not a decisive factor ... Wash-and-brush-up your face on occasion: because creams are rationed and soap is not.'

Prepared to make concessions over appearance in sacrificial wartime spirit, nevertheless *Vogue* was ready to take up cudgels when necessary. The line was firmly drawn in the August issue of 1942.

The beauty column made the concessions. 'Today, you want to look as if you thought less about your face than about what you have to face; less about your figure than about how much you can do. You want to look as if you cared about your looks, yes, but cared more about being able to do a full day's work - whether it be in a factory, on the land, coping with a day nursery, or just managing your home single-handed as so many of us do today. You want to look beautiful, certainly - what woman in what age hasn't wanted to? ... but you want it to be a beauty that doesn't jar with the times, a beauty that's heart-lifting not heart-breaking, a beauty that's beneficent but not beglamoured, and a beauty that's responsive - not a responsibility.'

But a special feature called It Must Go On inveighed against the rumour that the supply of cosmetics, already curtailed to 25 per cent of peacetime output, might be cut further. 'Cosmetics are as essential to a woman as a reasonable supply of tobacco is to a man. A welfare officer at a munitions factory said, "£1,000 worth of cosmetics, distributed among my girls, would please them more than £1,000 in cash" ... only when a woman looks her best can she feel and do her best. The supply should not be further reduced by prejudice or puritanism - more frivolous than the cosmetics they censure.'

The Second World War, unlike the First, brought no escapist follies, no fashion fantasies. They were impossible no less because of the wartime spirit than the government restrictions. In a speech to the Fashion Group of New York, Edna Woolman Chase, the American Editor-in-Chief, said, 'When people speak to me about this war they ask me "Isn't it going to be incredibly difficult to edit a luxury magazine like *Vogue* in times like these? Do you think that you can hope to survive?" My answer to that is - What kind of a magazine do they think this is? ... Fashions would not be fashions if they did not conform to the spirit and the needs and the restrictions of the current times.' Naturally, the fashion was for clumpy shoes, clumsy suits, box coats and headscarves tied into turbans hiding 'a multitude of pins'. Just as even wealthy women in the Depression were dressing down in plain black dresses and furless coats, fashionable

women were dressing in Utility-look suits or sweaters and slacks long before clothing restrictions. 'It looks wrong to look wealthy,' said *Vogue.* 'The woman well-dressed in the meaning of today would not easily be rendered helpless or ridiculous.'

From the outset of war the magazine took what Pearson Phillips, the journalist, has called 'a positive and optimistic line'. *Vogue* needed to take that line as early as October 1940, when in 'No margin for error', it discussed Sir Kingsley Wood's budget that slapped a new Purchase Tax on clothes. 'His acts might suggest him no friend to fashion; but *Vogue* (hopefully) detects an ally. Because of him, designers will get together frankly, to pool their ideas and use their limited materials to present a united fashion front. Because of him, women will buy carefully and cleverly ... by the inescapable pressure of the Purchase Tax he will set them practising those sound

dress maxims that *Vogue* has always preached. How often have we counselled against "the dress you buy and seldom wear" ... If women must buy less, they will buy better.'

Clothes rationing arrived in June 1941, by which time prices had nearly doubled in eighteen months. Coupons were distributed, and the rationing operated by a points system, a garment costing a number of coupon points irrespective of fabric and price. Utility clothes, however, fulfilled government requirements and sold at fixed prices. They were not subject to Purchase Tax. The Utility scheme involved at first 50 per cent and later 85 per cent of all cloth manufactured, controlling quality and price, and was reinforced by the Making of Clothes (Restrictions) Orders introduced in 1942, which covered nearly all clothing and restricted yardage and style. 'Dress restrictions simply pare away superfluities,' said

Vogue, making the best of things. 'The progress of the war has made it necessary to prohibit all superfluous material and superfluous labour ... Fashion is undergoing a compulsory course of slimming and simplification.' Readers were reminded, 'Subtraction, not addition, is the first of fashion rules - full liberty is liberty for excess as well as excellence.' On the other hand, 'The Board of Trade has now assessed our clothing requirements at 66 coupons - and margarine coupons at that - a horrid slight. It is now said that fashion's goose is properly cooked and done in, for want of the best butter. But fashion is indestructible and will survive even margarine coupons ... you cannot ration a sense of style.' Noël Coward's new leading lady, Judy Campbell, pointed out enthusiastically, 'Rationing is marvellous in one respect. You can make lack of money look like lack of coupons.'

Utility wear:
keeping healthy,
dressing sensibly

THE war was a watershed for fashion, forcing the development of a stable ready-to-wear structure capable of prosperous large-scale production in the fifties. 'The geniuses who invented the Utility scheme had a great say in the development of the fashion industry,' said Frederick Starke, a leader in the better off-the-peg market. By controlling quantities and prices the Utility scheme forced manufacturers to choose their cloths wisely and cut economically. Standards of manufacture were improved by

Satin and roses for export, striped cotton for home

minimum-standard government regulations and by a public forced by coupon rationing to discriminate, and methods of manufacture were streamlined and better mechanized by the pressures of rushed uniform production. Sizing and costing were for the first time regularized and accurately worked out, and labour was reassessed. The fashion industry's workers came out of the war more secure: they were paid guaranteed wages and conditions of work were laid down. When in July 1942 the government took over extra factory space for the storage of munitions and other wartime equipment, many manufacturers had to get together to stay in business. By 1947 Frederick Starke had formed the London Model House Group, seven leading manufacturers who united to establish the prestige of British fashion abroad, and to present a united front to buyers and suppliers. In 1950 the Apparel and Fashion Industry's Association was to say, 'a revolution has taken place behind the smokescreen of wartime conditions'.

Meanwhile, London's couturiers had managed their own revolution. Early in the war *Vogue* said, 'Paris is in eclipse, making it London's opportunity to shine. Already in London are the Paris houses of Molyneux, Paquin, Worth; lending all the prestige of their Paris connection to the drive for dollars. Creed, too, is here ... In England now, every branch of the fashion trade is stirring strongly. The challenge of the times has called forth, to admiration, qualities for which we have not always been conspicuous: initiative, speed, cooperation.'

In 1942 many of the couturiers were anxiously contemplating the possible next course of action of a government that had already introduced clothes rationing and the Utility scheme. There was just one way of proving London couture valuable to the national economy during the war, and that was export. The year before, nine couturiers had scored a success by cooperating in a special export drive, a collection for South America sent out under government auspices. *Vogue* had published a special South

'Inspired by Paris; worn in New York: why not in London?'

American edition to accompany the collection, and reproduced some of the photographs in British *Vogue*, where they looked conspicuously luxurious and glamorous among the regular diet of man-tailored tweeds and skimpy dresses. Norman Hartnell approached the managing director of Worth and other couturiers, urging a common front to the Board of Trade. Harry Yoxall, *Vogue*'s managing director, became the business head and entrepreneur of the new Incorporated Society of London Fashion Designers, aimed at developing the couture export market. The 'Inc Soc' was supported by fabric manufacturers and encouraged by the government. Early members were Norman Hartnell,

Peter Russell, Worth, Angèle Delanghe, Digby Morton, Hardy Amies, Creed, Molyneux and Michael Sherard. The first president was the Hon Mrs Reginald Fellowes, chief fashion personality of the early thirties, now camping in London in the basement of the Duff Coopers' house in Westminster.

In the spring of 1943, some well-designed, anonymous Utility clothes went into the market, the result of the Board of Trade's invitation to the couture to design basic garments subject to all the usual restrictions. Anne Scott-James had said, 'If Mayfair hasn't the skill to cut a good dress from three or four yards of material with five or six buttons it must learn - or go under.' Mayfair proved that it had.

FOR a magazine so closely concerned with Paris as *Vogue*, the blanket of silence that descended on the city during the Occupation was bound to change the character of the magazine, making it more insular but also more independent. Up to summer l940 *Vogue* ran a regular Paris Sidelights page, showing the character of the city essentially unchanged. Bettina Wilson wrote, 'Paris in the fifth month of the war is an attractive, comfortable, normal city with an intimate, almost country charm to life ... you can enjoy such luxuries as smart hats and plentiful taxis, but nobody will look at you askance if you go hatless or ride your bicycle on fine days. Hospitality in the home has practically become a cult - the war seems

Couture fittings and frivolous hats again

to have weakened, if not completely broken down, the impregnable barriers of French formality.' *Vogue* photographer, Arik Nepo, now a *poilu* in the French army, wrote, 'We're billeted in a barn. We tumbled in late one night, too tired to do anything but slump into the straw ... Next morning some cut pictures out of magazines and stuck them on the walls. *Vogue*, naturally, had pride of place - being full of pretty girls, divinely dressed; what more could you want?' From the Paris Ritz *Vogue* reported, 'Mrs Reginald Fellowes and her family, Madame Schiaparelli and her daughter Gogo, Lady Mendl, the Comtesse de Montgomery and Mrs Corrigan all live on the first floor. Dropping in for a drink means visiting from one room to the next, perhaps meeting the Sacha Guitrys, Mlle Chanel, Jean Cocteau, who also have

rooms there.' At Molyneux's mid-season collection there were Noël Coward, Madame la Générale Gamelin, and Mrs Fellowes - 'who knitted throughout the collection. There were four manniquins instead of fifteen, thirty models instead of a hundred, but those thirty struck clearly the informal note of the moment.' In poignant contrast to her circus ball of l938, there were Lady Mendl's Sunday lunch parties at Versailles - 'small tables covered with oil cloth, corn beef hash to eat, and guests take away the dishes and sweep up crumbs'. The soup kitchen for out-of-work writers and musicians had a first night opening with all the familiar faces: the artistic poor paid two or four francs, according to circumstances, the wealthy visitors twenty. Bettina Wilson wrote that the French were continually amazed by the fifteen-year-old look of the RAF pilots on their first Paris leaves, sitting in every *boîte* and tapping their fingers and toes to the music 'to which no one is allowed to dance in Paris, except at special galas', and told the story of the Lopez-Willshaws' furniture, which had been willed to the Louvre at the end of Monsieur's lifetime. During the first week of the war, a removals van drew into the courtyard with instructions from the curator of the Louvre to take the furniture away to a safe cellar for the duration, leaving the Lopez family sitting on the bamboo garden furniture in an empty salon.

There was grimmer news in July, when *Vogue* fashion artist Eric and his family left their home at Senlis, near Chantilly, to join a tide of refugees moving back from the German advance: as they left their house it was wrecked by a bomb. Seven months after the occupation of Paris, *Vogue* received a batch of pictures relayed from New York, showing a deserted Champs Elysées, a tide of bicycles and a cycle taxi, a cross between a sidecar and push bike. 'Across the great gulf of silence - and of misunderstanding, which we still believe cannot be turned to enmity between our peoples - come pictures of a strangely subdued city.'

During the Occupation some twenty of the famous couture houses managed to stay open in Paris, with or without their chief designers. Schiaparelli and Mainbocher went to America, where Mainbocher stayed, and Molyneux, Creed and Angèle Delanghe went to London. 'One of the first things the Germans did,' said Lucien Lelong, President of the Couture Syndicate, 'was to break into the Syndicate offices and seize all documents pertaining to the French export trade.' M. Lelong successfully resisted all German efforts to remove the couture lock, stock and barrel to Berlin and Vienna. 'I told them that *la couture* was not a transportable industry, such as bricklaying.' Thanks to his negotiations, the couture houses managed to show two abbreviated collections a year. 'A few months later, in l941 to be exact, due to the lack of materials, very severe restrictions were

ordered and textile cards with the point system started. We soon realised that if this regulation was applied to our great fashion houses, it would mean closing them down immediately.' M. Lelong renewed his discussions with the Germans and succeeded in obtaining exemption from point restrictions for twelve houses. 'Unfortunately, the Germans noticed at the end of six months that ninety-two houses were operating, which led to more discussions. Finally we succeeded in keeping sixty. Over a period of four years, we had fourteen official conferences with the Germans ... at four of them they announced that *la couture* was to be entirely suppressed, and each time we avoided the catastrophe. On another occasion, they demanded that 80 per cent of our workers go into war industries; this we managed to reduce to a 5 per cent quota, which in reality never exceeded 3 per cent.' He calculated that by the Liberation, 12,000 workers had been saved from unemployment and consequent labour in German war industries.

The export market was shut, and the couture had to depend on new clients, the recently moneyed class of black-marketeers, and many German wives, together with those of the Germans' French mistresses who dared to buy their clothes there. A great deal of subterfuge went on between the couturiers to get round German regulations. Bitter rivals in peacetime, they cooperated magnificently against the common enemy. When Madame Grès and Balenciaga were ordered to close their houses for two weeks because they had exceeded the authorized yardage for some of their models, the rest of the couture joined forces to finish their collections so that they could show on time.

Michel de Brunhoff, editor of French *Vogue*, was unable to publish it under the Germans. 'There was no honourable way; no way without compromise and collaboration. I stalled, and found slippery answers for the Germans when they suggested, and then ordered, that our magazines reopen with German backing.' Instead, M. de Brunhoff cooperated with *Le Figaro* to produce *Album de la Mode*, a magazine of the arts, theatre and fashion, from which *Vogue* reproduced some fashion pages after the Liberation.

THE Liberation of Paris appears in *Vogue* as a personal triumph. With exceptional speed, *Vogue* showed photographs of the fighting in October 1944 - fire and smoke, a priest encouraging boys at a barricade, General de Gaulle as he passed the windows of *Vogue*'s former Paris office. Lee Miller, *Vogue*'s *femme soldat*, went to check up on Picasso, 'generous and voluble as ever', Boris Kochno (Diaghilev's discovery) and Bébé Berard ('He has only one pair of trousers and has to wear an old trench coat as a skirt

to work in'), Paul Eluard and Michel de Brunhoff. Elsa Schiaparelli went back to Paris, found that food cost five to twenty times as much as it had in 1939, and resolved to give women 'clothes that they can live in, not parade in'. Cecil Beaton found Colette muffled up in bed with hot-water bottles and nine fountain pens, writing her memoirs, Gertrude Stein writing about G.I.s and Democracy, and noticed a hopeful sign: 'two actors with salmon-painted faces emerging from a jeweller's shop while a moving picture camera grinds' - the film industry had started up again. Lee Miller reported, 'There is one hairdresser in all Paris who can dry hair: Gervais (overleaf) ... He has rigged his dryers to stove pipes which pass through a furnace heated by rubble. The air is sent by fans turned by relay teams of boys riding a stationary tandem bicycle in the basement.'

In England, life was at its drabbest and most regimented. 'The penny plain of life is three farthings,' said *Vogue*, 'and the struggle to make up the difference takes so much of women's energy.' The public reaction to the Liberation fashion photographs - 'dazzling girls in full floating skirts, tiny waist-lines, top-heavy with built up pompadour front hair-dos and waving tresses; weighted to the ground with clumsy, fancy thick-soled wedge shoes' - was one of envious pique. *Vogue* sprang to the defence of Paris. 'If it surprises you to see pretty girls in pretty dresses, to see the beautiful clothes which the fashion houses never ceased to make, reflect that the life of France and her civilian technique of resistance must necessarily have been the reverse of England's. Here, it showed patriotism to obey regulations, to do the work required of us, to take no more than our rations. There, it showed patriotism to flout regulations, to avoid work except where it would not benefit the Germans (as in the luxury trades), to black-marketeer up to the hilt.'

The cultural life of Paris restarts. Vogue photographer Lee Miller encounters Picasso, above; editor of former French Vogue, Michel de Brunhoff, meets up with ex-Vogue artist, Jean Pagès; and Cocteau, Nush Eluard, Marcel Rochas and Bébé Berard celebrate over a wine-less lunch

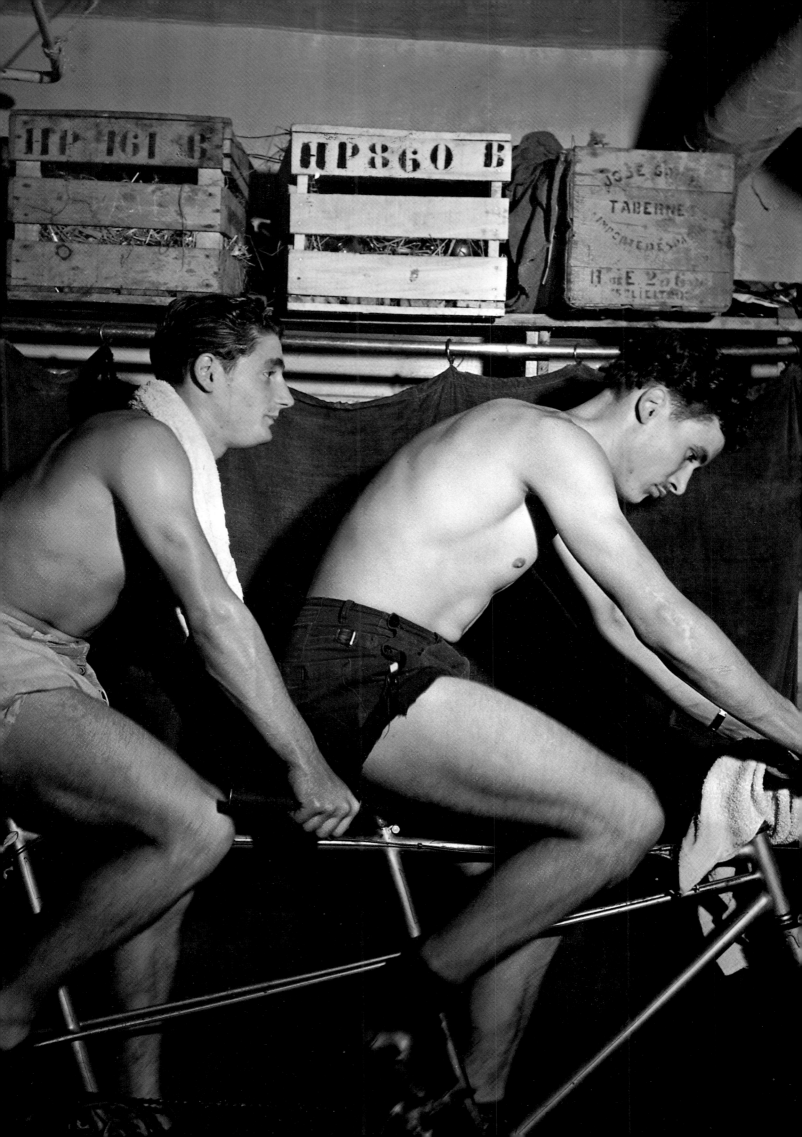

The Liberation allowed readers to see their first Paris collections for four years. The designs had a mixed reception. In America a ban was imposed on copying the full skirts and dressmaker details from photographs in fashion magazines. There was no question of being able to copy them here. In December, *Vogue* published a manifesto by Lucien Lelong, which amounted to an apology. 'It was only after the Autumn Collections were shown that I received copies of English and American dress restrictions, and I now understand why certain journalists found the Paris Collections exaggerated.

However, I must explain that my colleagues and I eliminated many models prepared before the Liberation - replacing them by simple suits and coats which we felt better suited the circumstances arising from France's official re-entry into the War at the side of the Allies.'

With the end of the war, clothes rationing tightened. There were shortages of everything from dried eggs to soap. Even bread was rationed, and the government spent £857,000 on a meat-substitute, an oily dull fish called snoek, which the press soon discovered was a large, ferocious cousin of the barracuda, which hissed and barked when annoyed. To give it a little much-needed glamour, the government published a series of snoek recipes, including 'Snoek Piquante'. However, nothing would make the public eat it, and at the time of the Festival of Britain a mysterious quantity of tinned fish came onto the market labelled 'Selected fish food for cats and kittens'.

The patient bearing with the minor horrors of war ended with the war. Now women were resentful of the shortages and restrictions: *Vogue*'s attitude changed from 'Dress restrictions simply pare away superfluities' to 'One has only to see a collection designed for export, and the same collection toned down to comply with austerity at home, to realize how much fashion value has been lost in the process.' In February 1946 *Vogue* invited a Cambridge economist and broadcaster, Louis Stanley, to explain why, after nine years without new curtains, linen, upholstery or pretty clothes, new goods were still unavailable. Stanley called his feature The Second Battle of Britain and said, 'It is bad enough when such goods do not exist, but to learn that they are being produced - the best this country can make - only not for domestic consumption is a bitter pill ... Women are further exasperated by illustrations in periodicals and the national press showing exotic fashions in Paris, Brussels, New York, Stockholm, even Germany,' and went on to explain, 'We have to wipe out a deficit of £1,200,000,000 from Britain's balance of trade.' *Vogue* jettisoned the positive and optimistic line on dress restrictions. 'It is unfair and economically unwise to leave our designers, one moment longer than is necessary, at such a disadvantage in relation to their competitors ... we add our voice to those which ask the Board of Trade to abolish austerity as soon as practicable ... and we hope that "as soon as practicable" will be construed with more urgency than it usually commands in Whitehall.' Marghanita Laski let fly: 'Patriotism is definitely NOT ENOUGH, and I, for one, am fed up. I'm fed up at home and I'm fed up when I go abroad. I don't like to see the foreigner pointing out a fellow-traveller (or could it be me?) and whispering. "You can see she's English - look at her clothes!" '

And yet no post-war look had evolved. James Laver, invited to make a prediction about the look to come, replied, 'Fashion has reached one of those turning points in history when everything may happen, just because anything may happen to the world. Neither in politics, nor in social life, nor in dress, nor in millinery are the lines yet laid down. We do not know yet *what* will get itself established.' One thing was certain, that the Board of Trade had created forbidden fruit and provided a violent psychological stimulus: women were eyeing clothes with passionate longing. When the New Look arrived, women were going to have it.

It arrived on 12 February 1947, at the freshly painted salon of a new young designer who had emerged from the ranks at Lucien Lelong. Christian Dior opened at 30 Avenue Montaigne, opposite, backed by Marcel Boussac, the textile millionaire, and at a stroke restored world confidence in Paris as fashion leader. The models swept in with fifteen, twenty-five, even eighty yards of fabric in their skirts, and spun up the aisle to the sounds of rustling petticoats and the crashing of ashtray stands. The New Look provoked extremes of delight in women, for whom each dress and suit was an orgy of all things most feminine and forbidden. Today no fashion innovation could equal the excitement of Dior's then, because it had been preceded by thirteen uninterrupted years of the square-shouldered Schiaparelli-initiated look.

DIOR said, 'I designed clothes for flower-like women, with rounded shoulders, full, feminine busts, and hand-span waists above enormous, spreading skirts.' His models looked absolutely different from the women in the audience. Dior's newly-designed woman had soft neat shoulders, a wasp waist, a bosom padded for extra curve, and hips that swelled over shells of cambric or taffeta worked into the lining: the dressmaking techniques were immensely complicated, some Victorian, some newly evolved. She walked leaning backward to make the hips more prominent, and her skirt burst into pleats, sometimes stitched over the hips or blossoming out under the stiff curved peplum of her jacket. Her hem rustled around some twelve inches from the floor, from which it was divided by the sheerest of silk stockings and the highest of pointed shoes. She was delicious, and she made all other women green with envy.

For *Vogue*, Dior's collection came at the end of a dull round of collections, too late to be justly dealt with in the March issue. There is a single line at the end of the Paris report, 'The season's sensation is the new house of Christian Dior - see next issue.' The April issue said, 'Christian Dior is the new name in Paris. With his first collection he not only shot into fame, but retrieved the general situation by ... "the Battle of the Marne of the couture."'

'His ideas were fresh and put over with great authority, his clothes were beautifully made, essentially Parisian, deeply feminine. Dior uses fabric lavishly in skirts - 15 yards in a woollen day dress, 25 yards in a short taffeta evening dress' and later, 'Fashion has moved decisively. Here are the inescapable changes. Always there is something prominent about the hips: in a shelf of peplum or a ledge of tucking; in bunched pleats or a bustle. The waist is breathtaking (except in the case of greatcoats). It is caught in with curved-to-the-form leather belts or wide, wide contrasting corselets or cummerbunds. Collars are clearly either/or: tiny or whoppers. Either way they are likely to stand up. Shoulders are gently natural. Sleeves are often pushed up; sometimes bulge at the wrists.' It was many years since the copy had been able to be so definite, so exact.

Women no sooner saw the New Look, but they had to have it. Dereta was one of the first off the mark in producing a grey flannel copy, and was taken aback to see 700 of them vanish from the rails of one West End shop within a fortnight. Naturally, because of the amount of fabric needed, the New Look could only appear in non-Utility clothes, of which production was limited. Yet manufacturers caught with large stocks of Utility 'man-tailored' suits lost money hand over fist: no one wanted them.

Sir Stafford Cripps summed up outraged official reaction: fury at the thwarting of fabric restrictions. He called a meeting of the British Guild of Creative Designers and suggested that they would be helping the national effort considerably if they would cooperate in keeping the short skirt popular - and the Guild obediently agreed to try. He then called in a committee of fashion journalists and, with the help of Harold Wilson, President of the Board of Trade, tried to persuade them to ignore Paris. They pointed out that their job was to report.

Several leading Labour party ladies including Mrs Bessie Braddock took up the struggle against what seemed to them to be a negation of all that women had won for themselves in two wars, making the classic mistake of thinking of female emancipation in male terms - that a woman has to be like a man to be free. To their attacks Christian Dior simply replied, 'I brought back the neglected art of pleasing.'

The New Look was such a success the new salon could hardly manage all their clients. I. Magnin took forty toiles, and Bergdorf Goodman, Bendel, Marshall Field, Eaton, Holt Renfrew took anything up to that number, ensuring that the whole of America would be wearing Dior or Dior copies. Buyers were still in the salon at two o'clock in the morning. The Dior staff worked eighteen hours a day. The two first famous customers were the Duchess of Windsor and Eva Peron, to be followed by Lady Marriott who ordered forty models a season, Mrs Thomas Biddle, who had each dress repeated in four colours, Mrs David Bruce and 'all those beautiful English women, victims of the currency restrictions in England' as the *première vendeuse* Suzanne Beguin put it - Lady Beatty, the Countess of Kenmare, Lady Peek ... and from Paris Baronne Alain de Rothschild, Madame Pièrre Michelin and the Brazilian-born Madame Martinez de Hoz, formerly Vionnet's favourite client.

Unknown to Sir Stafford Cripps, the press and Norman Hartnell, there was a private showing of Dior's collection to the Queen, Princess Margaret and the Duchess of Kent at the French embassy in the autumn. Princess Margaret in due course gave her seal of approval to the New Look by wearing it everywhere. The Queen and the Duchess of Kent were soon wearing the new length and line as it influenced their own designers, Hartnell and Molyneux.

Another new designer, Pierre Balmain, had opened immediately after the war. He was a contemporary of Christian Dior at Lelong - in fact, they shared a desk and had once discussed the possibility of opening a salon together. A friend of Gertrude Stein, he had won her affection by making for her and for Alice B. Toklas 'nice warm suits', and she wrote a charming small piece about him for *Vogue*. At his first collection, Gertrude Stein whispered to Miss Toklas, 'We are the only people here wearing Balmain's clothes, but we must not let anyone know for we are not great advertisements for the world of fashion.'

A feature of the war and post-war years were the enormous queues to get into anything that was on. It took the Blitz or the appalling freak winter of 1946-7 to keep them away. From 1945 to 1950, 20 million people a week were going to the cinema: as one manager said, 'You can open a can of sardines and there's a line waiting to get in.' Shakespeare enjoyed a tremendous wartime revival, embodying for the audiences patriotism, historical romance and a secure sense of tradition in one. The Old Vic was bombed and became hydra-headed, with its companies covering the entire country. London lost its position as cultural head of Britain as companies scattered, museums and galleries closed down and musicians went on tour. London's loss was England's gain, and the provincial towns were able to see the best actors and productions available. Noël Coward took his players on the road in 1942 with *Blithe Spirit*, *Present Laughter* and *This Happy Breed* - described by *Vogue* as '*Calvalcade* through the wrong end of opera glasses'. His first film was made at Denham with co-director David Lean. *In Which We Serve* was the story of a destroyer and the men who served on her, with Coward for the Captain, Celia Johnson as his wife, and Bernard Miles, Joyce Carey, John Mills and Kay Walsh in leading roles. It was notable for its realistic treatment of the subject, even down to a single swear word, and for its absence of condescension in dealing with the lower decks.

Whether it was Noël Coward and John Mills showing a stiff upper lip or Betty Grable and Rita Hayworth showing a bit of leg, films were a marvellous escape from reality. As *Vogue* said, 'Today's woman has less time to imagine, and a good deal of her imagining is done for her in the cinema.' Hollywood was earning about $70 million a year in this country when in 1947 the Chancellor of the Exchequer, at this moment Dr Hugh Dalton, slapped a customs duty of 75 per cent on the value of all imported films, the sum to be prepaid. The day after, the Motion Picture Association of America announced that all shipments of films were to be suspended immediately. Dr Dalton had blundered. True, he had presented the British film industry with the home market, but without the possibility of export to America, and much too soon - it was not yet ready to fill the gap. The improved standard of British wartime films - noted by *Vogue* in an optimistic feature called 'The coming heyday of British films' - was abandoned in the pressure to pour out cheap films to fill the cinemas. These were soon competing against the best American films that had been waiting for the embargo to be lifted, as it was a few months later by Harold Wilson as President of the Board of Trade. Rank lost over £6 million in four years. By the spring of 1949, seventeen out of twenty-six British studios were idle, and on top of that there was the crushing entertainment tax. British films had ceased to be a paying production. Laurence Olivier said, 'It is wrong to say that British films don't pay - they pay very well, but they pay the wrong people.'

During the war the BBC's staff trebled in size, due to the boom in sound broadcasting, which eventually reached virtually every adult in the country. It was not just the news, preceded by the booming notes of Big Ben, that attracted listeners, it was the radio show *I.T.M.A.* with Tommy Handley, the Minister of Aggravation and Mysteries in the Office of Twerps, the Mayor of Foaming at the Mouth, Funf the German spy ... *Much Binding in the Marsh* ... *Bandwagon* ... and in 1941 a different kind of programme, *Brains Trust*, with philosopher Cyril Joad and his shrill opening, 'It depends what you mean by ...', zoologist Julian Huxley, and retired naval officer A. B. Campbell, answering such questions as 'What is love?' and 'How do flies land on the ceiling?'

Elizabeth Bowen wrote about the function of the Third Programme for *Vogue*, stressing the need for drama writing on a high plane written specially for the air and commending Laurie Lee's *The Voyage of Magellan*, Louis MacNeice's *The Careerist* and Patric Dickinson's *The Wall of Troy*. 'To an extent, the programme is to create the listener: not less, the listener is to create the programme - by his response, mobility, curiosity, sensitiveness and willingness in approach to the not yet known. Third Programme is out to take long chances and risk wide shots.' She noticed with approval a new Europeanism of outlook, pointing out, 'We have an immense amount to catch up with. We need exactly the stimulus outside thought can supply.'

The museums reopened in 1945, and there were new foreign art books for sale in the book shops again. At the British Museum one of the first collections on show was the Sutton Hoo treasure, with an interesting tale behind it. Sutton Hoo's owner, Mrs Pretty, began in 1939 to have a persistent dream prompting her to open the barrow by the river. When, eventually, archaeologists broke into the mound they unearthed a huge Anglo-Saxon vessel bearing the richest series of funeral treasure ever unearthed in England - Byzantine silver dishes, enamelled flagons and jewels.

Orson Wells, 'married to Rita Hayworth: Delores del Rio chooses his ties'. Nöel Coward, above, the year of In Which We Serve

Overleaf: beauties of 1947; Vivien Leigh and ballerina Moira Shearer

DURING and after the Second World War, as after the First, there was a preoccupation with the nature of the role of women, the theme appearing and reappearing in *Vogue*, sometimes in captions, sometimes in features or odd remarks. Discussing the work of Frances Hodgkins, who died in 1947, Myfanwy Evans said, 'Many women who are creative artists of any kind manage to achieve their work in spite of the fact that they also live normal (if nerve-wrecked) lives as women, with husband, home, children, clothes, servants and so on; it is the intensity with which they can withdraw from the world at the time that they are working that makes them into amateurs or professionals; the degree to which they can bear to be so much in the wrong as to be thoroughly selfish, at times, that makes them good or indifferent artists ... a few take the most difficult way, and, remaining solitary, live or die by their work. Frances Hodgkins was one of these.' Anne Scott-James, reviewing *The Taming of the Shrew* at the rebuilt Old Vic, with Trevor Howard and Pat Burke, noticed, 'the Shrew was played like an honest child who grows into knowledge of guile and opportunism'. Again, Daphne du Maurier, opposite, writing in 1946 on doing nothing in the country: 'By this time I have had my bath, and am dressing, and am composing a letter to *The Times*, never published, on the subject of birth-control. The birthrate is falling, and I know why, and so do all the other women of my generation. It has nothing to do with insecurity or atom-bombs or the movies. It is because we don't *want* a lot of children, and had the women of past generations known how to limit their families they would have done so ... Why are the churches empty? Because, with modern warfare, hellfire holds no terror for us. And was it only fear of the hereafter that made my lady in her crinoline go to church three times on a Sunday? No, it was boredom.' The feeling in the air was defined and set out again by Simone de Beauvoir in *Femininity, the Trap*, which appeared in *Vogue* in July 1947: the leading disciple of Jean-Paul Sartre's Existentialist philosophy, she had already published three novels and a play.

In 1947 Edith Piaf sang at the music halls and Existentialism was the new word in Paris. *Vogue* followed Sartre from the bar of the Pont Royal Hotel - 'no Bohemian café. It is like a shining Ritz bar on the left bank, and here Sartre drinks dry Martinis' - to a lecture at the Sorbonne. 'Sartre, short, broad, about thirty-eight, with thick glasses, sat at a small table and talked about the theatre. He spoke with extraordinary clearness and force, without confusion or metaphysics, or trailing ends of Existentialism, or roundhouse sentences ... Speaking without notes and for one hour, he told these boys his theories about the theatre. His thesis is simply that the drama now must be one of situation and not of character. That life is a series of choices and the way one chooses determines one's character, not the other way around.'

Mid-way through the forties, Richard Busvine had written in *Vogue*, 'Television, as a medium of entertainment, will eventually kill sound broadcasting stone dead, just as the talkies killed silent films. This development is recognised by the experts as the natural and inevitable outcome of television progress, and they therefore await with considerable impatience official resumption of the Television Service.' It was resumed in 1946, but not looked forward to by everyone with the same enthusiasm as Richard Busvine's experts. There were growing fears that the future industrial development of England, of which television and fashion were a part, would detract from the quality of life. Would the Britain of the future be the same Britain that had been fought for? Siegfried Sassoon voiced these fears. 'Up to about thirty years ago it was still quite reasonable to say that God made the country and man made the town ... But the process of disfigurement has been insidious, because people accept it without realising the cumulative effect. These remarks are addressed (though only theoretically, I fear) to those who live in towns, but more especially to persons responsible for urban expansion, commercial exploitation of natural resources, and other energetic operations which can make a nice neighbourhood profitable and unpleasant ... While I write these words, the hedges of England are white with hawthorn; meadows are bright with buttercups and the golden foot of May is on the flowers. Bees rejoice in the blossoming chestnut trees; the cuckoo shouts all day at nothing ... One might almost believe that all's well with the world. But the urban and the rural district councillors think otherwise. For them a stretch of prime pasture land is an eligible building site; a leafy lane is a valuable road-frontage; and yonder copsy hillside has already been earmarked as the location for the latest thing in sewage farms. Next comes the county council road surveyor, companioned by an official from the Ministry of Transport who doesn't know an oak from an elm. Doomed are the delightful windings of the road Plumstead Episcopi to Crabtree Canonicorum.'

'The birthrate is falling, and I know why, and so do all the other women of my generation. It has nothing to do with insecurity or atom-bombs or the movies. It is because we don't *want* a lot of children...'

Fashion was never the same after the fifties. Fundamental changes occurred thick and fast to revolutionize the industry and take it into new territories, involving bigger business than ever before. For the first time, looks and lines assumed a universal importance, making headlines in the newspapers all through the decade. Fashion became a new language capable of subtle interpretation, when boys and girls between seventeen and twenty-three began to use clothes for group identification, provoking questions about fashion's role as signal, armour and decoration. For the first time in living memory, it was fashionable for men to be fashionable, a new preoccupation that cut right across society from the men about Mayfair to the Teddy Boys. New systems of mass production and the comparative prosperity of the late fifties turned the average Englishwoman into one of the best-dressed women in the world, and the introduction of nylon made it possible for working girls in the cities to wear white and pale colours every day. Teenagers opened up a whole new category in the fashion market, and the teenage art-school designers who turned their attention to non-establishment fashion produced totally original looks, the first fashion to begin at source instead of being superimposed from abroad or adapted. These were the formative fashion years of the century - the fashion-conscious fifties.

THE first ambition of the post-war years was to get back to normal. Britain was an almost bankrupt country faced with national shortages and a difficult balance of payments: austerity and rationing dragged on until 1954 in one form or another. The first sign of life had been women's appetite for the New Look, but on second sight its appeal was seen to be nostalgic, a reaction against the sexless clothes of wartime and the

drudgery of home and work without a man around. Now in 1951 there was a gesture of hope and confidence in the future. The Festival of Britain was the last fling of the Labour government, a nationwide celebration of the country's contribution to civilization and a demonstration of its potential in many fields. In London the main exhibition was to be built

on the blitzed South Bank site between Waterloo and Westminster bridges. The Festival Hall was the first building to be completed, a permanent fixture, and near it the Queen placed the stone for the future National Theatre. The bleak surrounding area began, under the organization of Gerald Barry and the designs of a team headed by Hugh Casson, to sprout pavilions and restaurants, constructions of cement and glass, striped awnings, flags and bunting, a Dome of Discovery with the largest unsupported roof in the world, and a towering Skylon which seems now to have

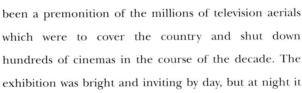

been a premonition of the millions of television aerials which were to cover the country and shut down hundreds of cinemas in the course of the decade. The exhibition was bright and inviting by day, but at night it came into its own, turning into what Michael Frayn called 'a floodlit dreamworld breathing music'. In *Vogue*'s eight-page Festival feature, leading off the Britannica issue, Marghanita Laski wrote, 'If all goes well ... what a country we shall live in, what a Britain we shall have! Through all our lifetimes, the man-made objects

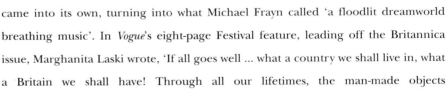

surrounding us have been devised, not to give visual pleasure, but unconsciously to assert that we are a

people wealthy, provident, puritan, insular, keeping our feet firmly on the ground and not liking to make ourselves conspicuous. Suddenly on the South Bank, we discover that, no longer wealthy, we can be imaginative and experimental and ingenious, colourful, gaudy and gay.' Proving her point, *Vogue* declared, 'The most fastidious and fashion-conscious woman can dress immediately for any occasion in ready-to-wear clothes' and proved it with fashion from Jaeger, Susan Small, Dereta, and Marcus, Brenner, Rima and Mary Black.

VOGUE gave the greatest emphasis all through the fifties to Paris, and for good reason. As the ready-to-wear market in America and Britain grew to giant proportions it depended more and more on Paris to act as authoritative pace-setter and to present new ideas that the public would recognize and look for in the shops. The fifties were a time of tyrannical dictatorship from Paris. Lines followed one another in quick succession: the envol line, the princess line, the tulip line, the I or H line, the A line, the trapeze line. It was a time when you couldn't be both fashionable and comfortable, unless you dressed at Chanel. You carried the weight of an enormous pyramid coat and you hobbled in pencil-slim skirts, always emphasized by photographing the model with one knee hidden behind the other. Collars turned up and bit into the chin, boned and strapless 'self-supporting' bodices made it difficult to bend, corsets pinched the waist and flattened the bust. 'Where has the waist gone?' asked *Vogue* in 1951, and answered, 'Anywhere but where you expect it.'

If you dressed in clothes from Paris or Paris copies, you wore stylized fashion with great but contrived glamour, geometric shapes, and exaggerated lines. Women obeyed Paris because of Christian Dior. No woman would forget during the fifties that a single collection had outdated everything in her wardrobe and made her self-conscious in a Utility suit. The consequence was that the fashion public were insecure, particularly about skirt lengths, and thought that every seasonal collection might bring a radical overnight change that would leave them with nothing to wear. Women M.P.s raged over 'short' skirts, and television news programmes quizzed women in the streets about what they thought of the new lengths. Hems were headline news.

The tyrannical dictator himself, Christian Dior, and his unrestricted yardage of tulle and satin at the Paris Opera

The build-up of public expectation exerted tremendous pressures on the Paris couturiers themselves. Although in fact no look could ever have the same effect as the New Look again - for first there would have to be no change for at least nine years - nevertheless the couturier trod a knife edge. Should the leading designers conflict too much in their lines, there was consternation and confusion among the buyers. Should they not change enough from the line of last season, buyers complained they were not being given a decisive lead. When Dior died of a heart attack in 1957, this public expectation was still intact. His 'dauphin', Yves Saint Laurent, was already signed up to a long and binding contract, and at the age of twenty-one found himself perched upon the multi-million franc edifice of the most influential fashion house in the world. He kept his balance with his first collection, when he launched the trapeze line: not too different from Dior's A line, but just different enough. In the salon people were trampled in the rush to embrace and congratulate him, and he had to appear like a king on the balcony to wave to the cheering crowds below. 'Saint Laurent has saved France!' said the French headlines. 'The great Dior tradition will continue!'

In the teeth of an unspoken agreement among the couture not to alter a hem length by more than two inches a season, Saint Laurent dropped the hem by three for his next collection. Twelve months later he bared the knees, and caused an uproar. A woman M.P. announced, 'I think it is ridiculous for a youth of twenty-three to try to dictate to sensible women. British women will not take any notice of this nonsense!' Radio programmes ran discussions on the likelihood of bare knees in Britain and one newspaper headline said, 'Dior's man can do what he likes. We won't show our knees!' *Vogue* presented his collection in the kindest light, ignoring the shortest skirts and showing his new hobble hem first in its 'least exaggerated ... utterly unalarming' form before leading up to the 'extreme trendsetter', and concluded, gallantly, 'When a new line is greeted with cries of indignation, it's a healthy sign ... it means that the fashion world is alive and kicking.'

It was at this difficult moment in his career that the army draft, three times deferred, wrenched Saint Laurent from Dior. After two months he suffered a nervous and physical collapse, recuperated, and returned to Dior to find his assistant, the thirty-five-year-old Marc Bohan, instated as chief designer. Saint Laurent sued and won £48,000 damages, which he used to open his own salon in 1962 with unqualified success and many of the staff from Dior.

Envol double-apron day dress by Dior

In 1949 Dior produced his envol line, previous page, superimposing a wing upon an arrow-thin sheath. His jackets flared at the back to jut over tubular skirts, his dresses had apron fronts that curved up to a peak at the back above pencil underskirts. His tightest skirt had to be split for walking, and from the waist, day and evening, he gathered flying panels.

Irving Penn's portrait of the Dior line in 1950, centre page, demonstrated the acceptable *Vogue* way to smoke - with head thrown back and a long cigarette holder. Dior's 1951 collection was his first without stiffened, padded interlinings. He launched his immediately successful princess line, left, with dresses fitted through the midriff, waist unmarked. The accompanying bloused jacket could be gathered into a wide belt at the hips and his new jumper suits with sailor collars fitted at the hips over flat pleated skirts.

In 1953 Dior reintroduced padding over the bust with his tulip line, left, and captured headlines by shortening skirts to sixteen inches from the ground - still two or three inches below the knee. Women were by now used to wearing skirts almost to their ankles, and were nervous of a change that might date their clothes as suddenly as the New Look did in 1947.

In 1955 Dior produced his new A line, a triangle widened from a small head and shoulders to a full pleated or stiffened hem above. He used stiff, strong fabrics such as tussore and faille. Variety came from the placing of the crossbar - high for an empire line, below fingertip level at its lowest.

Waists were raised by almost all the Paris dictators in 1956 bringing in a new suit with a cropped jacket showing a small cinched waist - above right at Dior - sarong dresses wrapped high to one side, and the innovation of a stiff four-inch waspie belt that had the effect of raising the waist and exaggerating the hips at the same time: it became the most copied accessory for years. Christian Dior's last collection left a legacy, the waistless shift or chemise dress that narrowed towards the hem, a refinement of Givenchy's 'sack', called the

'spindle' or 'chemmy dress', but soon known as the sac.

Left, Yves Saint Laurent 'on whom the Dior mantle falls: how he will wear it is the great fashion question mark,' wrote *Vogue* in 1957. The fragile *ingénue* made an enormous success of his first collection for Dior. Backbone of his collection was the trapeze, right, 'the most important and fully formulated line in Paris', flaring gently from narrow shoulders to a shorter wider hemline just covering the knees.

In his badly-received 1959 autumn collection, Yves Saint Laurent at Dior raised the skirt to the knees, belted every waist and pulled the skirt into a tight knee-band. The confidence invested in him the previous year was swept away by the outcry of the press, directed mainly at the skirt. 'At its simplest,' reported *Vogue* pacifically, 'it's no more than a tunic-effect ... in a larger-than-life more exaggerated version than will emerge as a final fashion form.'

IF Dior had personified the old Paris, Chanel stood for the new. Dior's death left Chanel, who reopened in 1954, the despot of the couture. Her success was due to her overwhelming appeal directly to the wearers of her clothes. Her unalterable convictions about clothes and what they should do for women produced a phenomenon unique in the fifties - an unmistakable Paris look complete from head to toe that was flattering, easy to wear, and did not date. The envol, the princess, the tulip and all the other lines had the date stamped indelibly across them. After a year, they were finished. Chanel's was a classic line, refined again and again but never fundamentally changed. The fashionable woman's motto for the end of the decade could have been 'When in doubt, wear a Chanel'. They were as comfortable as a cardigan, you could run in them, they had real pockets where you could keep your

The Chanel suit of the fifties, in jersey or checked tweed, would remain as wearable for forty years

cigarettes, and they gave a feeling of tremendous self- confidence.

In *Vogue*, the news of Chanel's return was the news of the year. In an exclusive interview before her first come-back Coco Chanel gave Dior and the other couturiers a characteristically caustic going-over. 'A dress must function or *on n'y tient pas*. Elegance in clothes means being able to move freely ... Look at today's dresses: strapless evening dresses cutting across a woman's front - nothing is uglier for a woman; boned horrors, that's what they are ... these heavy dresses that won't pack into aeroplane luggage, ridiculous. All these boned and corseted bodices - out with them. What's the good of going back to the rigidity of the corset? No servants - no good having dresses that must be ironed by a maid each time you put them on,' and concluding she rasped, 'I am no longer interested in dressing a few hundred women, private clients; I shall dress thousands.'

Opinion about her first collection was widely divided: she conceded nothing to the accepted stylization. *Vogue*'s cautious comment was 'At its best it has the easy livable look which is her great contribution to fashion history; at its worst it repeats the lines she made famous in the thirties; repeats rather than translates into contemporary terms.' By 1959 the contemporary terms had come into line with Chanel's convictions, and *Vogue*'s tone had changed completely. 'The heady idea that a woman should be more important than her clothes, which has been for almost forty years Chanel's philosophy, has now permeated the fashion world.'

Perhaps the most unusual thing about Chanel was that she never minded being copied. Unlike other couturiers, who banned publication of photographs of their collections until the buyers had time to produce authentic copies from toiles, Chanel allowed pictures to be shown immediately and was happy for the streets to be full of Chanel copies even if they did not put a penny in her pocket. In this she was not unlike Mary Quant, who said, 'The whole point of fashion is to make fashionable clothes available to everyone', but she also showed a supreme confidence that quality would prevail - that the real Chanel suit would be instantly discernible from all fakes.

I n the field of Parisian couture no designer ever rose so high as the Spanish fisherman's son, Cristobal Balenciaga, acknowledged as the greatest in his profession. He was a man with a calling far removed from the increasing commercial imperatives of the late fifties.

He was ambidextrous and could draw, cut, assemble and sew equally well with either hand. He worked with astonishing speed, putting together an entire garment in one sitting. Fabric and sleeves were his obsession. Courrèges and Gloria Guinness were to remember him working on a single sleeve for a night and a day without food or sleep. He hated publicity and never made headlines like Dior, but as the decades passed his enduring innovations could be appreciated at last. His clothes extrapolated from the body instead of following it, stylizing and abstracting the shape. For his sculptural evening dresses he used stiff paper taffetas blown up and rolled under into huge pumpkin skirts tipped up in the front, above, bows the size of umbrellas wrapping up tight sheaths, angles sharp as blades, and buoyant curving widths in the skirts.

His fox-collared tunic dress, opposite, had a black fox collar and a floating panel from collar to hem. Balenciaga's spring 1951 collection tipped the fashion balance in favour of a Chinese look, below left. Coolie hats framed flipped-up eyes and the wide barrel-shaped jackets were black over loose white gilets.

He put plenty of stiffening into jackets, cutting them to curve like shells over the body, and indicating the waist with a loose bow or an indented curve; his new midi line dropped the waist to the hips.

By 1958 Balenciaga and Givenchy had originated the 'high rise' waist - Balenciaga's dress, left, with a cape-like flying panel, cinching the ribs above an almond-shaped skirt narrowed at the hem. Bolero jackets were cropped to show the waist, and coats followed the same line when they were not flared into a trapeze.

Peruvian pink for a smock-straight Cardin town coat, 1958, above, and right,
a billowing kimono-sleeved moiré coat by Lanvin over tiered taffeta

In 1950, hair was pressed to the head and seldom seen in the day without a hat, eyes became 'doe eyes', with painted flick-ups of eyeliner at the outer corners, complexions were made pink and white, lips sharp and vivid. Collars were sharp, high and turned up, waists were minimized by girdles that gripped from rib cage to hips, peplums jutted out above the narrowest skirts. To make skirts look even narrower at the knee, models were photographed with one leg behind the other, and the new trumpet skirt which flared out again below the narrowest point turned full-length evening dresses into fishtail sheaths. The new shoe, day or evening, was the slingback with a rounded toe.

Dior's back-to-front day dress, 1948

By the middle of the decade, Audrey Hepburn was the best-known and most copied of all faces, and the classic Fiona Campbell-Walter was acknowledged as the most distinguished *Vogue* model.

The hat was half the point of any new look by 1957, usually a flowerpot toque pushed right down over the forehead, or a modified sou'wester with black veiling added or wrapping the

Audrey Hepburn, 1954, the year of Sabrina Fair

face in a mesh cage, with a rose topknot. Eyes and lips were heavily outlined, visible at a hundred yards, and exaggerated still more to show through veils. Long cigarette holders came back to keep the sparks away.

Irving Penn's 1952 photograph of the top twelve models, including magazine editors, a newspaper columnist, a singer and an actress

If America's influence was on the wane, it was because of a new generation of young British designers trained by the art schools into a practical knowledge of mass production, new methods of manufacture, sizing and grading, and production within limited price ranges. The Royal College of Art opened its School of Fashion Design in 1948, and its first professor of fashion was Madge Garland, a former fashion editor of *Vogue*. A long overdue acknowledgement of the kind of training needed, the school and similar departments throughout the country were quick to turn out uninhibited designs for non-establishment fashion. In 1953, the year *Vogue* started the regular Young Idea feature for girls between seventeen and twenty-five. R.C.A. students produced some original ideas for skirts: royal blue velveteen studded with silver buttons, turquoise felt slashed and slotted with velvet ribbon and tied with shoestrings, stovepipe trousers inside a double apron of glitter-scattered taffeta.

A product of art school, but not fashion school, was to give the young fashion movement its greatest impetus. Mary Quant, who failed to get her art teacher's diploma, was to be the 'major fashion force

Nylons - 'a wonderful new stretch ... a new fit-any-foot size' and, opposite, the nylon foundation garment

in the world outside Paris'. In 1955 she began her fashion career in the workrooms of Erik, the milliner, and in November she opened Bazaar in the King's Road, a joint venture with her future husband, Alexander Plunket-Greene. She began by buying clothes in, but could not find the kind of fashion she wanted. Within a few months she was designing her own clothes, although totally ignorant of how to set about it: she began by buying fabrics across the counter at Harrods because she didn't know that they could be obtained wholesale. She found that Bazaar was becoming a meeting place, a kind of 'nonstop cocktail party', and that the clothes were bought off the rails almost as soon as they had been put there. Her bedsitter was full of sewing women working until late at night to put dresses in the shop the next morning. A year after the Quant revolution had begun, nineteen-year-old John Stephen came down from Glasgow and opened his first shop for teenagers, moving it soon afterwards to Carnaby Street.

Other revolutions had provided the fabrics without which the looks of the fifties could never have taken shape. From the basic silk, wool and cotton available at the beginning of the century, there were in the fifties dozens of alternatives, most of them crease-resistant or permanently pleated, glazed, shrink-proof, water-proof, moth-proof, and washable. Synthetics had begun to appear in fashion during the thirties, with Schiaparelli's 'Rhodophane' dress, and there was a cheap rayon or 'art silk'. By 1938 there were Lastex tops and an improved, uncrushable rayon, but it was not until the war, which had so many beneficial effects on the fashion industry, that textile manufacturers were forced back on their resources, and made the most of them. Nylon transformed the fifties wardrobe, making the petticoats that stood up by themselves and the almost invisible 12-denier stockings, the fake furs and the permanently pleated nightdresses, the laces and the knitting yarns. In 1954 *Vogue* published a glossary of man-made fibres including acetate, Dynel, Fibrolane, Orlon, rayon and Terylene. 'Putting on clean clothes daily,' as Madge Garland pointed out in her book *Fashion*, 'once thought to be an eccentricity of the Empress Josephine, is an habitual occurrence in the life of any girl.' Washable drip-dry clothes passed into the fashion repertoire of working city girls. Thick pullovers were made for the first time in powder blues and primrose yellows with Orlon and Courtelle; foundation garments were revolutionized, nylon fabrics in great variety making possible the two-way stretch doll-size girdle of 1952. Four years later one firm, English Rose, had ninety garments in their range, an increase of sixty since 1950, a number made possible by the different kinds of synthetic fibre.

THE fifties were the time when women went out to work as a matter of course. In the 1920s when Van Dongen had painted The Lady Wants No Children the question had been 'job or children?': in the fifties women were prepared to take on two jobs in order to have the best of both worlds. By the end of the decade, more than half the married women of Britain were going out to work. But T. W. Higginson could still have said, as he had nearly 100 years before, 'Like Charles Lamb, who atoned for coming late to the office in the morning by going away early

'Any time we girls have to go to work the result, historically, is that we do things better than the opposite sex. I mean gentlemen will go to all the trouble of keeping office hours and holding Board Meetings and getting Mr Gallup to make a poll, and sending their Public Relations agents to Washington, in order to reach a decision which any blonde could reach while she was refurbishing her lipstick'

Anita Loos, 'Decline and Fall of Blondes' *Vogue* 1951

in the afternoon, we have, first, half educated women, and then, to restore the balance, only half paid them.' A girl might earn about three-quarters of a man's wage, doing the same job in industry. And even when she was granted equal pay, did she get equal opportunities? Out of 150 top jobs in the BBC, only four were held by women. One of the two women governors, Mrs Thelma Cazalet-Keir, said, 'The BBC conceded equal pay for women as long ago as 1926, but what's the good of that if no women get paid at the top level?' Jacqueline Wheldon, wife of BBC producer Hew Wheldon, complained about the tone of voice in which television programmes

addressed women, 'that jolly welfare-worker air, and that special sort of voice, as though every woman sitting at home was a moron ... the term they used for us in the studio, I believe, was a "Mums".'

The publishing of Christabel Pankhurst's memoirs, *Unshackled*, provoked in *Vogue* a spirited debate between political commentator Henry Fairlie of the *Spectator* and *Daily Mail*, and working women. Mr Fairlie wrote that women were really reluctant victors in the battle for independence, and that they were the victims of a confidence trick by an industrial society to supply a cheap new source of labour. He declared that the typewriter had re-enslaved women, 'few of whom are happy until they have had a baby', and that cosmetics, fashion, and women's magazines were all 'drugs to keep the slaves quiet'. In reply, Jean Mann, a J.P., invited Mr Fairlie to accompany her to the factories 'and look at the "exploited". They have wages and hours fixed by the Trade Unions. Ask these women if they would prefer their pre-emancipation jobs as servants, charwomen, cleaners, washerwomen!'

Dame Sybil Thorndike said, 'If we are better persons as a result of freedom how can we have lost as women?' Margaret Casson, architect, drew attention to his 'curious assumption that because women are physically constructed to bear children they are therefore mentally and emotionally bound to enjoy domesticity above every other kind of life', and Shirley Conran, fabric designer, said, 'I chose to work because I found housekeeping easy and boring and because my husband is more interested in me as a fellow worker than as a super servant. What would Mr Fairlie rather we did when our children are past the baby stage? Embroider radiator screens?' Penelope Mortimer spoke for many working women when she said, summing up, 'Thoughtlessly, often effortlessly, one somehow manages to retain the affection and attention of one's family while voting, typing, earning. Even (and this is more remarkable) while cooking, cleaning the bottoms of saucepans, and administering Syrup of Figs. Could it be that, although a woman, one is a human being?'

The new word of the fifties was 'media'. Television had brought the meaning home to 26 million people by 1959, Aldous Huxley's 'television fodder', most of whom had been initiated by the televising of

Young Idea: pinafore for the office, £4 9s 6d

the Coronation and had gone out to sign hire purchase agreements afterwards. The opening up of this enormous exploitable market came with Commercial Television in 1955, 'a national disaster', according to the Labour party. So much was talked about 'subliminal' advertising that people began to doubt their own powers of resistance. In 1958 *Vogue* was writing, 'Having got ourselves thoroughly fussed about subliminal advertising and motivational research - the profitable quarrying of the depth-boys - we might return to ground level and look at the not so deep ideas employed upon our consciousness. The latest thought in cereal packages, expected here from America, is a celluloid gramophone record that can be cut out of the side of the package. Our sample performed, piercingly, "Goofy's Space-Trip to the Moon". "There's a big future for this little gimmick," say the instigators. "Birthday cards that sing *Happy Birthday*, aspirins with lullaby jingles!"'

In the new wave of commercialism, *Vogue*'s editorial policy moved closer to the fashion industry, introducing an annual advertising award for good design, a colour range to help sell the new seasonal ranges in the shops, *Vogue* endorsements for featured fashions, and an attempt to catch the attention of specific markets and perform a reader's service in the introduction of Mrs Exeter in 1949 and Young Idea in 1953.

After a pilot in 1945, *Vogue* initiated an annual talent contest with a first prize of £50 and the offer of a job. This competition still operates today. Early winners included Cynthia Judah, Penelope Gilliatt, Anne Sharpley, Anne Scott-James, Isabel Quigly, Jill Butterfield and Edward Lucie-Smith. In 1952 the model competition began: 'Don't think, because no whistled tributes are forthcoming from corner boys, that you can't be a model.' In case of discouragement from family, *Vogue* added, 'you can reassure your father, your husband or your son, on one point: modelling is terribly respectable. Whatever you do, you will always be exemplarily clothed, and excessively chaperoned - by a photographer, photographer's assistant, fashion editor (*stickler* for form), fashion editor's secretary and studio girl.'

IF Englishwomen of the fifties had never been better dressed, the men had never been so fashion-conscious either. In the prime P. G. Wodehouse years, a well-dressed man's appearance had to be remarkably inconspicuous - like Lord Emsworth, indistinguishable from his gardener - an inclination encouraged by rationing during the war when men had given up their clothing coupons to their wives and become shabbier than ever. After the war, attitudes began to change. The nostalgia which had provoked the New Look and made its success inevitable also affected men's fashion. Men-about-Mayfair began to dress in a way that owed something to Edwardian fashion, and by 1950 the look had evolved completely: curly bowlers and single-breasted coats with velvet collars and ticket pockets, trousers narrowed almost to drainpipes, and a rolled-up umbrella. The shirts they wore were striped, with the stripes running horizontally, and with stiff white collars. Suits had four-button jackets left undone over waistcoats with small lapels, some in rich velvet patterns. Recording the fashion, *Vogue*

drew attention to the fact that bowlers had become almost a uniform again since the recent order of the general commanding the London district that they should be worn by ex-Guards officers and Guards officers in civilian clothes. The four men *Vogue* photographed, Peter Coats, William Aykroyd, Mark Gilbey, opposite, and Michael Chantry-Inchbald, were surprised to find within a year or two that they and their friends had been the inspiration for the Teddy Boys of South London, who adapted the single-breasting and velvet collars, the ticket pockets and loose fit into their own aggressively stylish look. The Teds wore plain white shirts with the collar turned up, or a bootlace tie, a silver chain round neck and wrist, a tattooed forearm and fingers, a thick draped suit and crêpe-soled brothel-creepers. Their hair was worn long and immaculately set in quiffs and sideboards, but greasy: Teddy Boys would go to a barber for 'styling', but drew the line at having it washed or dried under the dryer. For the first time the young had a fashion identity of their own.

Tommy Steele, right, the year of 'Never Felt More Like Singing the Blues'

THE word 'teenager' itself was an import from America - a country where girls of six went regularly to the hairdresser and wore make-up at nine. Before the war there had been only 'girls' and 'youths'. Their independence was based on their earning capacity. A popular song was 'You gotta have something in the bank, Frank', and by l958 the average wage was £8 a week for a boy, £6 for a girl: together just a living wage. There were jobs, shorter working hours, and somewhere to go afterwards. For the teenager in the mid-fifties there were jazz clubs, where students in 'wild-beast' sweaters jived with a girl in one hand and a bottle in the other, dance halls with a skiffle group or a rock 'n' roll band playing Bill Haley's *Rock around the clock*, clubs where juke boxes were fed by leather boys in black jeans and jackboots and studded jackets, and all day there were coffee bars, a refuge behind a bamboo grill overgrown with ivy and philodendron. Soon the West End was covered with Espressos, Wimpys, Bar-B-Ques, Moo-Cow Milk Bars and Chicken Inns.

and tight jeans, or a tight sweater and a full skirt over layers of crackling petticoats. Towards the end of the fifties an art student look came into fashion with donkey jackets, falling-down hair, slim striped skirts, and a basket over the arm.

These were the first fashions that began in the street and worked upward into *Vogue*, and by l959 the magazine was asking questions about the new trends. 'What does fashion represent? Decoration? Armour? A mood of society? For millions of working teenagers now, clothes like these are the biggest pastime in life: a symbol of independence, and the fraternity-mark of an age-group ... The origins of the teenage look are urban and working class ... and it has been taken up with alacrity by the King's Road. Contrariwise, it is itself influenced by the romantic concept of Chelsea.' By now, this look was growing out of English soil. America might have invented teenagers, but London was dressing them. As *Vogue* said, the look 'owes nothing to Paris or Savile Row; something to entertainment idols (the Tommy Steele haircut ... the Bardot sex babe look); much to Italy, and surprisingly little to America (apart from a suggestion of the mechanized cowboy about motor cycling clothes): which may well be a symptom of a growing indifference to the American image'.

The States were doing so well by the mid-fifties with separates and coordinates from California - shirtwaisters and dirndls billowing out over drip-dry nylon petticoats, blue jeans derived from Levi Strauss's work pants for gold prospectors - that the French couture sent out a committee to study production methods, and returned surprised and impressed.

More teenagers in Britain bought the 'sweater girl' bra, with its conical stiffened cups spiralled with stitching, than the copies of Dior's 'ban the bosom' corsets in l954. In pursuit of a Jane Russell bosom, girls bought a California bra - one was called the 'Hollywood Maxwell' - or shortened their shoulder straps and chanted the dormitory rhyme, 'I must, I must, achieve a bigger bust. I will, I will, make it bigger still. Hoorah, hoorah, I need a bigger bra.'

Among the teenagers, it was the men's clothes rather than the girls' that identified the group, whether it was the Italian jacket, the fluorescent socks and the winkle-pickers of the East Enders or the shaggy sweaters, beards and sandals of the 'weekend beats'. It was a reversal of *Vogue*'s world in which women wore the conspicuous fashions and men formed the decorous background. The girls from any of the groups might wear a buttoned cardigan with a string of beads and a narrow skirt, or a Sloppy Jo

The technical age increased *Vogue*'s scope in several directions. On the features pages you might find a photograph of the new German Mopetta, a car no larger than a big shopping basket, or a photograph of a pink daffodil or a blue-tinted rose ... 'no garden need now be without a yellow peony if you can spell Mlokosewitschii'. A picture of an experimental British Railways carriage, complete with reclining tweed seats, double glazed windows and thermostatic fan heating, might be paired with a new plastic greenhouse which allowed more ultra-violet light than did glass, or details of the new transatlantic telephone cable and what it might do for readers' calls to Australia.

The technological revolution meant a new kind of fashion photograph, taken with telephoto lens, and unforgettable pictures by photographers of the calibre of Irving Penn and Snowdon, experimenting with the greater freedom given by sophisticated equipment.

Penn's, usually lifts from American *Vogue*, are of superb quality, to which end he would fly a planeload of electronic equipment across the ocean to the particular room he wanted to work in, or smash to pieces an imperfect camera rather than have it adjusted. Unlike Penn, Norman Parkinson preferred to work out of doors, and said, 'A studio is like an operating theatre. You go there to get part of yourself removed.' He took his models into the fields, below, and introduced a new degree of realism to the regular coverage of country clothes. First day in a foreign country with a dress to photograph, he would tell the driver, 'Take the first right and the second left, the first right, the second left, until I tell you to stop,' until 'the picture arrives'.

Snowdon's, then Antony Armstrong-Jones's fashion pictures were outrageous moments caught by the camera when no one should have been looking - a girl teeters and falls into a river, fully dressed, a woman knocks over a couple of glasses as she rushes to embrace a man, above, the tide creeps up to cover the knees of a girl who has fallen asleep on a deckchair.

Common to the photographers who found their feet in the fifties was the independence and assurance of the model, who seemed to own the clothes and be carrying on her own life regardless of the camera, unless she faced it with a disconcerting new awareness.

SHE called her grandfather Grandpapa England, but she was only third in succession. She never went to school but was brought up, according to her mother's precepts, 'to spend as long as possible in the open air, to enjoy to the full the pleasures of the country, to be able to dance and draw and appreciate music, to acquire good manners and perfect deportment and to cultivate all the distinctively feminine graces'. It did not seem likely that she would ever be nearer to the throne, until her uncle abdicated. On 2 June 1952, in Westminster Abbey, she became Elizabeth the Second, by the Grace of God of the United Kingdom of Great Britain and Northern Ireland and of her other Realms and Territories, Queen, Head of the Commonwealth, Defender of the Faith. The occasion went off perfectly except for torrential rain

which soaked the 300,000 people who slept along the processional route on the night before. In the morning they were doubly rewarded in seeing their young Queen, and by the news that Everest had been climbed. On her silver jubilee the Queen was to say 'When I was twenty-one I pledged my life to the service of our people and I asked for God's help to make good that vow. Although that vow was made in my salad days when I was green in judgement I do not regret nor retract one word of it.'

Cecil Beaton photographed the Maids of Honour: from left to right, Lady Anne Coke, Lady Jane Heathcote-Drummond-Willoughby, Lady Rosemary Spencer-Churchill, Lady Moyra Hamilton and Lady Jane Vane-Tempest-Stewart.

VOGUE opened out into new territory with its features pages, edited by Siriol Hugh Jones then by Penelope Gilliatt, who was to marry John Osborne. Maria Callas faced James Dean across the pages; Gina Lollobrigida, 'the new Italian bombshell', jostled Joan Littlewood, 'a forthright genius with a band of idealists who toured the country in a lorry, clinging to the belief that the theatre is a popular art'; Satyajit Ray with his 'rapt fidelity, his realism and silence' lined up with Lady Docker and her new gold-plated, zebra-upholstered Daimler. *Vogue* heard Liberace pronounce, 'It is good when fans get behind the life of a star who's a good clean citizen with a fine family life', and reported Mike Todd's words: 'Now what about these cinemas? Save a lot of time if I had them both. Call 'em Liz's First House and Liz's Palace.' *Look Back in Anger* was described as 'the play that gave tongue to a generation scarcely

deterioration of a seedy music hall performer. Reviewing John Braine's *Room at the Top* in its filmed version directed by Jack Clayton, the story of an anti-hero's climb through the British class system, Penelope Gilliatt wrote admiringly of what was dubbed 'kitchen-sink realism': 'Casually the camera-work states what a Northern town is like: cobbled streets, smudged views of chimneys, women cooking at ranges, wet slaps of washing to be dodged by children playing in the street. I know that remarking on this must sound like applauding a dress for being sufficiently in touch with reality to have a zip, but it is notable in our cinema.'

The anti-hero also loomed large in Hollywood. Siriol Hugh Jones wrote, 'In the broad shoulders, the slouch, the regional accents and the beautiful broad peasant features of Richard Burton, the inescapable animal bulk of Marlon Brando, the neurotic-baker-boy puzzlement of Montgomery Cliff, the sulking pout of Farley Granger - there lies glamour, there lies the heroic touch, the dream of 1952.' The heroine, whatever nationality, often had a new childishness - there was more than a hint of the schoolgirl in Audrey Hepburn, of the baby in Marilyn Monroe and Brigitte Bardot.

The beginning of a new male cult was first noticed in 1952. 'The changing order of heroes is identified along the hair-line,' said *Vogue*. ' "Pre-war hair" was innocent of evil communications with brilliantine and other base messes. The post-war look is that of the crew-cut and its dire derivatives.'

The anti-hero who behaves disgracefully, but on whose side we're on anyway, was not only a figure of British novels and plays but of the new Hollywood films, which now produced the masculine brute rebellion

Idols and images: Maria Callas, who was to say 'First I lost weight, then I lost my voice, then I lost Onassis.' Marlon Brando, whose performance in Streetcar Named Desire would be copied by generations of actors. Overleaf: Pablo Picasso at Antibes and Francis Bacon in London: Dylan Thomas, on the publication of Death and Entrances, and Alec Guinness at bay in Feydeau's Hotel Paradiso

speaking to its elders', the film *Gigi* as having produced the feeling that you were being sold something subliminally - 'M.G.M. good evenings start with Colette'. Penelope Gilliatt was quick to feel the tinge of 'Ealing-tight-little-island humour' in Alec Guinness's *The Horse's Mouth*. She asked Sidney Nolan what he thought of the performance. 'Very good,' he said. 'People usually play artists as though they were mad.' 'But, Sidney,' said his wife, 'this man was completely nutty.' 'Don't be silly,' said Nolan. 'He behaved just like I do.'

The new writers' disillusion with British politics and cant, system of privilege and genteel complacency gave the old order a rough time from 1954, when Kingsley Amis published *Lucky Jim*. Osborne's *Look Back in Anger* at the Royal Court, with Alan Bates and Mary Ure, shocked people into self-awareness and marked a turning point in the decade, but it was in *The Entertainer* that he parodied most cruelly the decline of England through the

It was not surprising that the popular hero should have changed in a decade when people became insecure as quickly as they became self-aware. Bertrand Russell spoke of 'a fated and predetermined march towards disaster' and Sir Julian Huxley saw over-population as the gravest threat to man's future. Meanwhile, hideous dormitory suburbs and bleak, boring new towns spread out to ruin the countryside in place of the glittering cities that had been visualized in the twenties. Not even the material prosperity of the late fifties could gloss over the disasters of Suez and Hungary, Korea, mistrust of politics and feelings of panic about the future that culminated in the Aldermaston marches and the demonstrations of civil disobedience. Television was the main factor in the new awareness, bringing the facts and the action of world affairs into the private lives of 26 million British viewers by 1950; no wonder the public was more involved and more anxious than it had ever been before.

'London is a city of and for the young,' wrote Peter Laurie in *Vogue* in 1964. 'Probably no other in the world offers us the opportunities that are here. Wherever enthusiasm, energy, iconoclasm or any kind of creative ability are needed, you'll find people in their mid-twenties or younger.' Britain had emerged from the turbulent last years of the fifties a changed country. 'In that period,' said American journalist John Crosby, writing for the *Daily Telegraph* colour supplement, 'youth captured this ancient island and took command in a country where youth had always before been kept properly in its place. Suddenly the young own the town.'

actors and model girls, pop artists, hairdressers, interior decorators, writers and designers. They came from all kinds of backgrounds. For instance, a cross-section of half a dozen, numbering David Bailey, Terence Donovan, Tony Armstrong-Jones, Alexander Plunket-Greene, Michael Caine and Terence Stamp, includes sons of an East Ham tailor, a Mile End lorry driver, an East End tugboat captain, a Billingsgate fishporter, a Q.C., and an organist. Because their prestige was founded on their talent, they shared a fierce respect for professionalism and treated any kind of amateurishness with contempt. Aggressively self-confident, any of them could have said in the words of Andrew Oldham, when joint manager of the Rolling Stones, 'I don't have to depend on other people's talents to get me on. I am good enough myself. I am good and I am going to get better.' There were no pretensions. When David Bailey published his *Box of Pin Ups*, designed by Mark Boxer and written by Francis Wyndham, he described the beginning of his career like this: 'I had a choice at this time, aged sixteen, time Monday, 4.30 in the afternoon. I could either be a jazz musician, an actor, or a car thief ... They - from Mars or wherever they are - said I wouldn't be a fashion photographer because I didn't have my head in a cloud of pink chiffon. They forgot about one thing. I love to look at all women.' It was a feast for the press when he married French film star Catherine Deneuve in 1965, and the *Evening Standard* wrote, 'The bridegroom wore a light blue sweater ... and light green corduroy trousers', 'the bride arrived smoking' and the best man, Mick Jagger, 'arrived with a blue denim suit and blue shirt with no tie'.

Baby Jane Holzer, wealthy jetsetter and Warhol companion. Opposite, Mick Jagger in 1964. Below left, Terence Stamp, and right, Lord Snowdon and his Aston Martin: more affordable, the great British minicar, previous page

Everyone in the country who read the colour supplements or watched television could tell you who in particular owned the town, how they lived and the names of their friends. Yet the new social order was unrecognizable to members of the old establishment like Loelia, Duchess of Westminster, who told *Vogue*, 'London Society is a world which for better or worse no longer exists'. There was a new class system, and by the mid-sixties even *Private Eye* was referring - with disdain - to 'the new aristocracy'. They were all young, talented and concerned with the creation of 'image': pop singers, photographers,

At every level, the sixties were a time of the young doing what they wanted better and more profitably than had been done before; a time of round pegs in round holes. Mary Quant had 'weathered the storm for the young designers' and in every field there were new opportunities to make revolutionary changes. Even in what had been the most reactionary circles, power was in the hands of the young. Roy Strong, below, talking to *Vogue* in 1967, 'very young (at thirty-two) to be the new Director of the National Portrait Gallery', was planning the first photographic exhibition in the museum's history. 'The great thing that all galleries have had to learn is that you have to go out to your public ... Everybody's got it fixed in their mind that the National Portrait Gallery is terribly dull and dowdy, which, indeed, it was. Now the ordinary chap is coming in off the streets and saying, "Heavens, this is interesting, this is enjoyable."'

One thing Britain lacked, and felt the need of, was a young, dynamic political leader to fit the revolution, such as the USA had in President Kennedy, opposite. Between 1960 and 1963 the standing of Macmillan's government was falling sharply, and a note of envy surfaced in *Vogue*, voiced by Mary Holland, who referred to America's 'new leader whose youth, vitality and firecracker energy make European statesmen seem like tired Victorians', and to 'the rest of us who still have old men at the top'. *Vogue* also took a great interest in the President's wife, Jacqueline Kennedy, who had won American *Vogue*'s talent contest in 1951 when, in answer to a question about People I Wish I Had Known, she had chosen Baudelaire, Oscar Wilde and Diaghilev. The good-looking and clothes-conscious Mrs Kennedy 'has resolutely eschewed the bunfight and the honky-tonk of the American political scene and is inclined, instead, to the gentler practice of painting, conversation, literature and fashion.'

Quite soon the youth cult was blown up out of all proportion by thousands of features in the magazines and newspapers. Arthur Jones, writing about the mods and mids in *Vogue*, said as early as 1964, 'There *is* a teenage society, there are new standards in England that are not quite local nor Standard English; but the whole hopeful, dynamic thing is frozen by the gorgon stare of the old, the rich, the powerful.' There was also a new language invented by and for the teenagers: not the 'pad', 'Daddy-oh' and 'real gone' that issued from the American teenagers, but, using Arthur Jones's examples, 'Tone, nip up the G's and con the drummer for some charge so we can have a circus before charp.'

In the middle sixties *Vogue* ran headlines like 'The World Suddenly Wants to Copy the Way We Look. In New York it's the London Look, in Paris it's Le Style Anglais ... Where fashion influence came from Hollywood, the Left Bank and Italian films, English girls now not only have the nerve to be themselves but can enjoy watching others copy them.' Britain had a new image all round. America's attention had been caught by British theatrical talent since Osborne's *Look Back in Anger* had been voted the best foreign play of the season on Broadway in 1958. Since then there had been plays by Brendan Behan, Lionel Bart, Robert Bolt and Shelagh Delaney, the tremendous success of *Beyond the Fringe* and the Establishment team, and Anthony Newley's *Stop The World, I Want to Get Off*. New York critics were talking about a 'British domination of Broadway'. At the 1963 Paris Biennale it was British artists who had stolen the thunder, particularly David Hockney, Peter Blake, Peter Phillips and Allen Jones, all from the Royal College of Art. When David Hockney's exhibition opened in New York the next year, it was sold out on the first day. The same year, Dame Margot Fonteyn and Rudolf Nureyev of the Royal Ballet dancing in Vienna received an ovation that beat all records, with eighty-nine curtain calls. Britain was no longer a respectable bowler-hatted gentleman with a stiff upper lip: the last remnants of that image had been dissolved for ever by the Profumo affair.

More than anything, it was the phenomenal success of the Beatles' American tour within a year of President Kennedy's assassination that put anything British on top. When they arrived at Kennedy Airport the whole country became Beatle-obsessed. Hardly anyone noticed when Sir Alec Douglas-Home arrived there five days later. In March, American advance sales for the sixth record, *Can't Buy Me Love*, were 2 million, and the next month they held not only the first five places in the American Top Hundred, but also the first two places in the LP charts. If what Andrew Oldham, below, said was true, pop music was taking the place of religion and the Beatles were gods. America's supreme accolade was to give them Carnegie Hall for the first pop concert in its history; England's, perhaps, was the serious evaluation by *The Times*' music critic, who said, among other things, 'one gets the impression that they think simultaneously of harmony and melody, so firmly are the major tonic

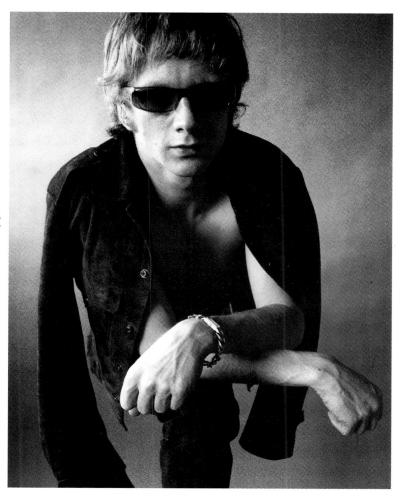

'Britain was no longer a respectable bowler-hatted gentleman with a stiff upper lip: the last remnants of that image had been dissolved for ever by the Profumo affair'

sevenths and ninths built into their tunes, and the flat submediant key switches, so natural is the Aeolian cadence at the end of *Not a Second Time*' (the chord progression which ends Mahler's *Song of the Earth*) and admired 'the exhilarating and often quasi-instrumental vocal duetting, sometimes in scat or in falsetto, behind the melodic line; the melismas with altered vowels ("I saw her yesterday-ee-ay") which have not quite become mannered.'

OUR other most popular export, the mini skirt, officially arrived in New York in 1965 with a British fashion show arranged by the Fashion House Group and held on board the *Queen Elizabeth*. The models in their thigh-high dresses stopped traffic on Broadway and in Times Square, and were seen on television all across the USA. Mary Quant, opposite, made a fortune there the same year when she took thirty outfits on a whistle-stop tour of twelve cities in fourteen days, the models showing the clothes to a non-stop dance routine and pop music. She soon had a business worth a million pounds, selling to the USA, France, and nearly every other country in the Western world, designing twenty-eight collections a year. She received her O.B.E. for services to the fashion industry in 1966, and went to Buckingham Palace in a mini skirt.

Both the designers and the wearers were enjoying a new form of expression. The outlets were the pop-playing boutiques, packed with clothes ideas by and for the young. In 1960 an American girl fresh from campus told *Vogue*, 'I had a sort of idea things might be a bit stodgy here, but I couldn't have been more wrong. I have to put my hands in my pockets when I go around - especially all those small boutiques in Chelsea and Kensington.' You could try on as many clothes as you liked without being intimidated or reproached if you didn't buy: in fact it was sometimes difficult to find the assistant if you did want to buy. You never knew what you would find in a boutique. Seasonal cycles of stock were disrupted, and new looks arrived as soon as outworkers could get them finished, sometimes a few days after they had been designed. Girls who wanted to have first look at weekend stock learned to go along on a Friday evening when the boutiques took delivery and stayed open late. The fifteen- to nineteen-year-olds that had been a tiny fraction of the buying market in the mid-fifties grew in number until, in 1967, they were buying about half of all the coats, dresses, knits and skirts sold in the country. By then, to add to the deluge of ideas from home-grown designers, boutiques were selling every unusual thing in the world that you could wear, from rough Greek wool sweaters to saris; kimonos to harem pants; caftans to half-cured sheepskins from Turkey and Afghanistan. The fashion categories of the fifties, 'formal' and 'casual', had ceased to have any meaning. In 1960 *Vogue* photographed Mary Quant's dark striped pinafore with a black sweater for day, and on its own for going out to dinner. By 1965, the women at any smart party would be divided into two groups: half in the shortest skirts, half in full-length evening dresses, and neither feeling out of place.

One boutique that stood out from the rest because of its immediate popularity was Biba. Its originator and fashion designer, Barbara Hulanicki, right, began the original mail-order business in 1964,

calling it after her sister. Her husband, Stephen Fitz-Simon, directed all the business aspects and ran the Biba empire. As a boutique, Biba started in undistinguished two-room premises off Kensington High Street. What made it different from the start was its dark, exotic, glittering interior, jumbled with clothes, feathers, beads and Lurex, spilling out over the counters like treasure in a cave. Its gimmick was the incredible cheapness of the clothes. There were no price tickets, but the poorest student could afford to say 'I'll have it' before asking 'How much?' In 1966, for £15, the price of a Mary Quant party dress, you could walk out of Biba in a new coat, dress, shoes, petticoat and hat. Stephen Fitz-Simon said, 'We could always spot a member of the trade turning a dress inside out to see how it was possible

to sell it for so little.' Biba was often so crowded on a Saturday that there would be a queue waiting to be let in one by one as customers left, and Barbara Hulanicki remembered, 'We had to go out every day with a damp cloth to wipe the nose marks off the window.' By the end of the sixties the clothes were no longer so cheap and Biba was an all-in-one store, but it had more than a gimmick; it had an immediately recognizable style of its own. Derived from the mood rather than the nuts-and-bolts of Art Nouveau and Art Deco, Biba set a precedent for two decades or more. Design companies like Laura Ashley and Ralph Lauren would learn to construct an entire landscape of lifestyle around a particular product. The sixties made Britain into a fashion leader and the most inventive country in the world. A million and one young designers were spilling out of the art schools, bursting with new ideas and practical expertise. As *Vogue* said in 1962, in a feature called Fresh Air in the Rag Trade: 'For the first time the young people are making and promoting the clothes they naturally like: clothes which are relevant to the way they live ... ours is the

clothes were meticulously controlled, demure, and revealed every line of the body. Zandra Rhodes finally found at Fortnum & Mason the freedom to extend her prints into clothes, making floating chiffons and crinoline nets coloured with a painter's palette. Woollands 21 Shop, under the guidance of Vanessa Denza gave a boost to many of the best designers, including the remarkable Ossie Clark, who made them a special collection while he was still at the Royal College of Art. Many, too, went to the best chain fashion shops such as Wallis: Jeffrey Wallis was a key figure in the recognition and promotion of British designing talent. He had already made the Chanel suit almost a uniform among well-off working women, and had kept the distinction and comfort of these suits by using the identical fabrics that Chanel had chosen. Equating good design with good profits, he told *Vogue*, 'The rise of positive thought that's strongly and independently creative is one of the most exciting things that's happened in England. Today a market exists of around 5 million people in America, Europe and England all on the same fashion wavelength.

Mary Quant through the sixties: from left to right, 1963, '66, '65 and '60

first generation that can express itself on its own terms.' As David Bond put it, 'I design clothes I'd like to see my girl friends in.' An unprecedented flow of talent was coming from the Royal College of Art under the aegis of Professor Janey Ironside - Zandra Rhodes, Marion Foale and Sally Tuffin, Bill Gibb, Ossie Clark, Graham Smith, Christopher McDonnell, Anthony Price, 'She taught by the tone of her voice,' said Graham Smith. 'She never told us that something was terrible. She didn't have to. She gave us the know-how and then left us the greatest freedom.' Not all the talent went into the boutiques. Jean Muir, for instance, our leading classic fashion designer, went to Jaeger for six years, and was backed by Courtaulds when she opened as Jane & Jane in 1962. She emerged independently with a unique standard in line and proportion - her

Today the provinces are places like Texas, not Manchester. Young designers are springing up all the time: industry is creating the climate for them, top buyers the right type of background.'

Meanwhile in the face of this tremendous competition, the British couture was shrinking. In 1966 when they numbered seven, the hard facts were that a suit, with three fittings, came to between £90 and £200: a best-seller would not exceed an edition of twenty-five. Even Michael, who dressed the most Parisian-minded of London's couture market, would have found it difficult had he not had an arrangement with Marks & Spencer, supervising their fashion design. Here and in Paris the couture began to turn to boutiques and ready-to-wear - Nina Ricci, Yves Saint Laurent, Cardin and Lanvin among others.

CHOOSING fashion photography over a career as a jazz musician or car thief, David Bailey walked into *Vogue* in summer 1960 and changed fashion pictures into portraits full of sexual imagery. The momentous first meeting with Jean Shrimpton took place in the studio where Brian Duffy was photographing Shrimpton for a cornflakes advertisement. 'He was taking the picture against a blue background' remembers Bailey. 'It was like her blue eyes were just holes drilled through her head to the paper behind. Duffy said "Forget it! She's too posh for you" and I thought, we'll see about that.'

Within a few months Bailey's camera had turned Shrimpton - a self-effacing country girl who apologized if you bumped into her and hated to walk down the street alone in case someone stared - into a sex icon as desirable as Monroe, Taylor or Bardot. *Vogue* models had usually been photographed standing aloof in smart city streets or country houses. Now Jean Shrimpton sprawled on the floor, skirts thigh-high, sometimes toying with a gun or cuddling a teddy bear. For the first time *Vogue*'s fashion pages were torn out to become pin-ups in bars and garages.

Today David Bailey is one of the most distinguished British photographers. He is married with two children and spends much of his time making successful commercials. Jean Shrimpton is married, too, and runs a pleasant country hotel. But in some ways neither will ever be able to escape the other. Bailey and Shrimpton were the sixties, just as much as the Beatles and Mary Quant.

THE boy from Oswaldtwistle came to London in 1961 on a wave of talented northerners spearheaded by David Hockney. Clever, working-class, subversive, they were dedicated to their work and brilliantly entertaining. At the Royal College of Art his skills blossomed in a talented class under the inspired tutelage of Professor Janey Ironside, head of the fashion school, and Bernard Nevill, the distinguished textile designer. Determined that his finals show was going to leave an indelible memory, Ossie Clark returned from a trip across the USA with David Hockney carrying a roll of black and white striped silk twill, and before the phrase 'op art' had been coined, he dressed his models in dazzling mini-length quilted stripes, one in a full-length coat with electric light bulbs switched on round the collar. He

was the only student of his year to be awarded a first-class degree, and his first collection for Quorum sold outright to Henri Bendell of New York.

In the heady sixties, Ossie Clark was precisely where it was at - in Santa Monica with Hockney, in New York with Andy Warhol and Jimi Hendrix, at Reddish House with Cecil Beaton, in Villefranche with Mick and Bianca. His shows on a houseboat, in the Aretusa or at the Royal Court in London were carnivals, his clothes - many of the most beautiful in fabrics by his wife, Celia Birtwell - sex incarnate, Beatles and Stones in the audience, Amanda Lear and Patti Boyd modelling. Deprived in the fifties, rocketed to fashion stardom in the sixties, over-indulged in the seventies and broken like a butterfly in the eighties, Ossie Clark, even bankrupt, is still the best we have.

Red Indian leather, satin and silk cut by Ossie Clark, below left, with prints by Celia Birtwell. On singer Julie Driscoll, opposite, cream and brown pyjamas, on Mrs George Harrison, below right, scarfed red, blue and white chiffon with handkerchief points

In 1963, the year of the Profumo affair and Beatlemania, all the new looks were tied up with Vidal Sassoon's important new haircut - very hard, very architectural, a thick chopped bob that was shaped to bare the top of the neck, or fall a little longer in limp curves, straight as silk. Vidal Sassoon's talk of bone structure and head shape led to rethinking in make-up and a new interest in hats. *Vogue* talked of rouge being used not so much for colour as 'contouring the cheekbones', and James Wedge designed a collection of hats to go with the Sassoon cuts, sold from boutiques in the hair salons. Boo Field Reid made more anti-establishment hats, including Bardot headscarves, Jules et Jim caps, and tweed baseball caps. The newest shape was the helmet fitting the head like a bathing cap, with a chin strap, in white fur by James Wedge, in black satin with a cartwheel brim by Dior. Herbert Johnson were selling as many bowlers to women as to men, in stitched dark velvets.

False eyelashes were an essential part of make-up, and wigs began to edge into the fashion picture. Most hairdressers were telling their staff to cut down on back combing and advising clients to buy false pieces instead. Everyone wanted more hair, adding thickness and height,

whether the cut was short and bobbed or long, heavy and swinging. Lipsticks paled down and disappeared as eye make-up became heavier and harder.

'Brevity,' said *Vogue* 'is the soul of fashion.' Dresses shrank in all directions as the micro-skirt reached an all-time high in 1966. Cut-outs and mesh inserts revealed the midriff, necks were scooped, and see-through crochet dresses over 'body-stockings' appeared to reveal a bit of everything.

In the summer you went bare-legged and rouged your knees. In the winter you covered your exposed limbs in thick patterned tights or stretch lace, and boots climbed up the legs in pursuit of hemlines.

'Boots, boots and more boots are marching up and down like seven leaguers,' said *Vogue*, 'taking with them stockings and kneesocks in thick depths of textures.'

1964 was the year of Courrèges. An expert tailor trained at Balenciaga, he had been producing his own collections since 1961, but with his spring show he suddenly came to the front of the Paris couture. To the throbbing of tom-toms in his hot white showroom on the avenue Kleber he paraded clothes that seemed to be the projection of a space age far ahead.

Vogue said, 'White sets the pace at Courrèges - tweeds, gloves, kid boots, shoes, tunics, coats, trousers are all white. Trouser suits are lean, the trousers curved up at the ankle in front, dipped over the heel at the back; overblouses are straight and squarish, jackets single breasted with a back half-belt; skirts are the shortest in Paris - above the knee. Coats are seven-eighths.' From now on sixties fashion would revolve round bare knees, the trouser suit, outsize sunglasses, white leather boots, white and silver.

'Courrèges clothes are so beautiful,' said Andy Warhol. 'Everyone should look the same. Dressed in silver. Silver doesn't look like anything. It merges into everything. Costumes should be worn during the day with lots of make-up.'

Nearly all designers became infected with the mirage of 'space age fashion'. Cardin's dresses were half sculptures, little shifts suspended from ring collars, or cut out discs and squares. Saint Laurent made his shifts in sheer organza, transparent except where they were striped or chevroned with silver sequins. Ossie Clark was to design the space-shuttle hostesses' clinical helmeted white uniforms for Kubrick's *2001*, and in the cheaper ready-to-wear all the new jackets were made of silver leather or shirred silver nylon. Everywhere, from the couture to the ready-to-wear, the favourite dress was the briefest triangle, taking no account of the waist. It was worn with the shortest hair - Leonard cut Twiggy's right back to the skull, shorter than a little boy's - huge plastic disc earrings, silver or white stockings, silver shoes laced up the leg and bangles of clear plastic and chrome.

Helmets, boots and plastics of 1964. James Wedge's leather cap, opposite. 'Courrèges invents the moon girl', below left, and Paco Rabanne revives chain mail in featherweight paillettes, below right

BY 1967 fashion had finished with the 'space age' look, and designers began to see the future in terms of the present again. The pop revolution burnt out with a crackle of paper dresses. Expendable clothing came in poster prints or fabric patterns, in packs costing from 16*s*. to 22*s*. 6*d*. Biba sold a silver paper suit for £3, and there was a metal-sprayed Melinex dress that wouldn't rip, tear, flare, crack or scratch, but it made such a noise that you could hear it in the next room. Geometric haircuts, creaking welded plastics, silver and chalk white had become almost a uniform.

Fashion had embraced brutalism and gone off at a wild tangent. Now, in sharp reaction, there was a passion for the most romantic of dressing-up clothes. There were three schools of fashion - flower-power, ethnic, and *Viva Maria* ruffles and ringlets. Hippy fashion was endorsed by Yves Saint Laurent's gypsy print shifts or peasant looks with ethnic kerchiefs covering the hair.

The musical *Hair* arrived in London and emphasized the alternative to Vidal Sassoon:

'Long, beautiful, gleaming, steaming, flaxen, waxen, curly, fuzzy, naggy, shaggy, ratty, matty, oily, greasy, fleecy, down-to-there hair like Jesus wore it halleluyah, I adore it HAIR!'

Face and body painting were a feature of the late 1960s. No one did it better or more often than America's surreal top model, Verushka, opposite, a tall and beautiful German countess. The most frequently photographed *Vogue* exponents of the hippy school were Penelope Tree, below right, and Patti Boyd, otherwise Mrs George Harrison, with her Red Indian leather fringes, headbands, and colour mixtures in layers - a sort of rag dressing mixed with bells, tassels and tinsel. The jetset version of this look were the wealthy gipsies that poured out of the London boutiques and special store departments in every variety of gaudy finery: plumes, hand-painted silks and boots, Ukrainian wedding dresses, Moroccan caftans, Indian pantaloons and Afghan sheepskins.

'On gusts of balalaika music from the Balkans, from hurdy-gurdy gypsy camps in Varna and the Ukraine, from straw-roofed Chechen villages, comes pure theatre for evening fashion,' said *Vogue*. 'Give full reign to instincts for display and munificence with tinselled finery, brilliant skirts, silk embroidery, gold lace, tall boots, pattern used with pattern.'

Hand-painting flowed over face, body and clothes, eyelashes were lengthened and thickened and hair was twisted with hanks of nylon or plaited like a Red Indian's

THE scope of the fashion revolution can be seen at a glance in men's clothes. From the revival of Edwardian dandyism in the fifties via longer hair, printed shirts and no ties, polo-neck sweaters and skintight jeans. By the end of the sixties men had moved on to satin, chiffon, frills and lace. Mick Jagger donned a white organdie dress (with trousers) for an open air concert, and the mods wore high heels, with handbags and plucked eyebrows. Even the men who had changed their appearance least had changed a lot. Plain grey suits turned out close at hand to be made of rainbow weaves. 'Hooray Henrys' wore sheepskins, cavalry twills and paisley cravats: their trousers were cut in a slim backward curve, and their trouser hems were cut to lift over the instep. John Taylor of the *Tailor and Cutter* attributed it all to sex: 'It's simple; men want to look younger and more attractive now. England is not such a man's world as it was.' *Vogue* attributed it to women: 'The hand that rocks the cradle is at last having some influence on the droopy fawn cardigan and the grey socks round the ankle', and found that 'The Englishman's view that to be at all dandified is effete - or worse - is changing. After-shave lotions are established, deodorants a necessary commonplace, and colognes are catching on.' Fancy dress reached its height in 1968, when Christopher Gibbs urged *Vogue* readers to buy and wear the Diaghilev ballet costumes being auctioned at Sotheby's: 'There is nothing wrong in loving young men (though loving everyone is where it's at) ... I'm sure Diaghilev would have been delighted to see his extravaganzas clothing the supple limbs of young Voguesters, bringing a pinch of the glory of All the Russias to dowdy gimcrack London ... Come in colours, and the grey pox will never catch you. Heed only the poets and the painters and you'll never go wrong.'

Terence Stamp, above, restaurateur, with his restaurant manager Rex Tilt. The 'Trencherman' was 'down the far end of the King's Road ... where London becomes English again after Contemporary Living and West Coast manqué'

RUNNING away from the grey pox was a recurring theme of the decade. When Kenneth Tynan donated the name satire to the humour of *Beyond the Fringe*, a university review on the outskirts of the Edinburgh Festival in 1960, he remarked, 'England is complacent and the young are bored. There is the desire to hear breaking glass.' Humour had grown up since the days of the rollicking moon-mad Goons, and soon improved the quality of newspaper and magazine writing, too. Peter Laurie was not entirely free of satirical intent himself when he wrote in *Vogue* that satire was 'a new journalistic commodity in vogue among the cultured press.' He pointed out that the Angry Young Men had quickly exhausted the value of sheer protest, but had, in the process, uncovered a mine of social material which they had scarcely had time to work. Jonathan Miller said that the English seemed unable to be funny in their own voices, but in turning their attention to the target instead of the audience, the satirists found a new lightness of touch. 'There is an assumption that we are moderately well read and moderately familiar with what more serious artists and thinkers are doing,' said Peter Laurie, and Mary Holland wrote about *That Was The Week That Was* as 'this anarchic, unkind, uneven and often downright sick arrival to BBC television ... It is certainly not well-intentioned. It is sharp-tongued, cruel, sophisticated, and, praise be, firm in its belief that the audience is as clever as itself and capable of enjoying the same jokes.' Satire depended on a supply of targets ripe for sustained attack, and as these fell away towards the end of the sixties, this particular vein ran dry.

Beyond the Fringe's Jonathan Miller, opposite, and Dudley Moore, right, with Jean Shrimpton

Overleaf: Jeanne Moreau, the sadder-but-wiser French heroine of Jules et Jim and La Notte, and the Swedish Britt Ekland, starlet and wife of Peter Sellers

Opposite, John Osborne, standing, and Albert Finney. Below left, Fellini, director of La Dolce Vita and 8¹/₂, and, right, Jean-Luc Godard of the nouvelle vague

Following pages: Peter Sellers, 'the greatest comedian since Chaplin', and Jane Birkin, who made her first film appearance in Blow Up before London lost her to Paris

IN the cinema, the decade began with long queues for foreign films. Londoners lost their interest in Cinerama, Todd A-O and Cinemascope, and went instead to the *nouvelle vague* films of Louis Malle, Claude Chabrol and Jean-Luc Godard, or the new Antonioni or Fellini from Italy. 'In the windy chill of London's Westbourne Grove,' said *Vogue* in 1960, 'people queue past the baker's shop and down the side street to see *Hiroshima Mon Amour*. There are four shows a day, all packed; no seats are bookable and the telephone is permanently engaged. With this, his first feature film, director Alain Resnais joins the ranks of the new French film-makers who make us stand in line while many cinemas are half empty.' Resnais followed up with *Last Year in Marienbad*, developing the use of flashbacks to introduce the past into the present and give a feeling of *déjà vu*. Foreign films had a great influence on British directors, and the birth of neo-realistic films like Karel Reisz's *Saturday Night and Sunday Morning*, produced by John Osborne's and

Tony Richardson's Woodfall Films. 'With this film,' said Francis Wyndham, 'the British cinema has really grown up at last, indeed one might argue that this is the first British film ever made. It is about working class life today.' There followed a remarkable series of British films including *A Taste of Honey, The Loneliness of the Long Distance Runner, A Kind of Loving* and *Billy Liar*. Directors of all nationalities were aware of each other's work and films became much more cosmopolitan. To take three key films of the sixties, Richard Lester's Beatles vehicle *A Hard Day's Night* and Joseph Losey's sinister *The Servant*, with brilliant performances by Dirk Bogarde and James Fox, were both made by Americans living and working in England, and Antonioni's *Blow-Up* - about a fashion photographer remarkably like David Bailey - by an Italian in London. A characteristic of the sixties was the fantasy fulfilment theme followed by a nightmarish ending - as in *Jules et Jim, Lolita* and *Bonnie and Clyde*.

'To those who say, "what was good enough for my father is good enough for me,"' said the catalogue of the John Moores Liverpool exhibition, 'modern methods will not commend themselves in art as well as in transportation or heating.' After the 'British painting of the Sixties' show at the Whitechapel, Edward Lucie-Smith introduced the work of a handful of dissimilar painters to *Vogue* readers and explained how wariness, toughness, worldliness and a scrupulous professionalism were now part of an artist's equipment. David Hockney, he said, 'has had the good fortune to find himself at the head of a well-defined new school of painting - the so-called "Pop Art" movement. What nobody seems to have noticed is that Hockney is at his best just where he is least closely affiliated to Pop ... he is a true narrative painter.' Howard Hodgkin was 'representative of a more sober kind of figurative painting ... the nearest thing to a really classical artist'. Eschewing fashion in a fashion magazine, he told readers to look at a painting they would like to buy and see it as it would look in ten years' time - 1973 - 'just at the moment when it is most out of fashion, most *déjà vu*'. When *Vogue* interviewed Andy Warhol in 1965 he was more interested in Minimalism than Pop, and delivered to Polly Devlin a non-interview to go with his intentionally empty art-works. 'Edie is with us,' he informed her. 'The film with Edie for the festival is very beautiful. Half of it's out of focus and she does nothing ... I flick on the switch and the film makes itself ... Movies are so boring and you can sit and watch mine and think about yourself or whatever you want to think about. I don't know what I'm doing either. It keeps us busy.' He ventured that Tennessee Williams had written a script for him: 'Really only a title. It's "F and S". That's all. He wrote it. I'll make a film of it when I get back.' 'What does it mean?' 'What does it mean to you?' Does Warhol collect anything himself? 'All this art is finished ... Squares on the wall. Shapes on the floor. Emptiness. Empty rooms ... Redundant. That's what my art is all about.'

A year later, Elaine Dundy interviewed another celebrity of the sixties, Tom Wolfe, whose *Kandy-Kolored Tangerine-Flake Streamline Baby* arrived in England via Jonathan Cape. His way of writing, his feud with the *New Yorker* and his extravagant form of dress had made him a V.I.P in the USA, and here he had a considerable impact on journalism, particularly on magazine and advertising copywriting. The new Wild Man of American literature, he had savagely attacked the *New Yorker* style, 'which requires that whenever you mention, say, an actor's name, you give the play he was in at the time, the cast, the theatre, and the length of time it ran and you get a fact-stuffed sentence that's quite beside the point ... People only write in careful flowing sentences. They don't think that way and

they don't talk that way.' Elaine Dundy described his clothes - a pale grey sharkskin suit and a tie twice as wide as usual with clowns dancing on it ... 'It is necessary to refer to his clothes because he ascribes almost magical properties to them. "If that shirt and that shirt were running a race," he will say, pointing

to what appear to be two identical shirts, "that shirt would win."' His style was hyperbolic, colloquial and immediate.

> I shall burst this placid pink shell
> I shall wake up slightly hungover,
> Favoured, adored, worshipped and clamoured for.
> I shall raise Hell and be a real
> Cut-up.

'The idea of what is news today is still a nineteenth-century concept,' he said. 'Perfect Journalism would deal constantly with one subject: Status.'

Opposite, Andy Warhol, at thirty-five: 'All this art is finished ...'
David Hockney, back from California with swimming pool pictures in 1965

AN ideal subject for Tom Wolfe to have written about, Penelope Tree, opposite, combined the extreme youth, hippy glamour and snob appeal that spelt high status by the end of the sixties. She was seventeen when David Bailey first photographed her for *Vogue*, and soon moved in with him to his all-black house in Primrose Hill. Brought up in New York, Barbados and Florence, her shy manner and fey silences obscured her background as the daughter of a billionaire banker and a mother who was a US Ambassador to the United Nations. Penelope Tree installed a UFO detector in Bailey's drawing room and filled the house with self-styled musicians and poets, the Black Panthers and a Tibetan holy man; the party went on twenty-four hours a day until the sixties fizzled out.

The dynamic turmoil of the late fifties and early sixties had become the nervous stimulation of the mid-sixties. In reaction to the orgy of commercialism that had charact-erized the decade, there was the alternative society of the idealists, the flower people using words like 'love' and 'freedom' in a woolly way. But it soon became evident that the alternative society was just as ripe for exploitation as any other. Underground magazines were paid for by record advertisements. *Hair* ('What do you want to be, besides dishevelled?') supposedly genuinely hippy, had an advance ticket sale of $250,000. In the USA flower-power was turning ugly in the heat of anti-Vietnam agitation: among the serious demonstrators were every kind of provocative revolutionary. In London the hippies found they could not live and buy pot by making candles and Batik prints alone. Rather than take National Assistance, a few dropped out and went to farm in the remotest parts of the country. For the most responsible and constructive thinkers - the Des Wilsons and the Naders - the conclusion seemed to be that we must do the best we can with what we have, working from inside the system to redress the balance and make good. With exploding populations and shrinking resources, the question already was, 'Is it too late?'

In the USA flower-power was turning ugly in the heat of anti-Vietnam agitation: among the serious demonstrators were every kind of provocative revolutionary

That women were deeply uncertain of their place in the world was to become increasingly evident by the mid-seventies. In the meantime, fashion displayed as in a crystal ball the confusions of the female role. Retro-mania filled wardrobes with fleamarket sequins and feathers while in clubs such as Canvey Island's Gold Mine, boys in short-sleeved shirts and girls with forties perms, red lipstick and platform shoes danced to Glen Miller. Mainstream fashion dressed women in several visible layers, short skirts over long, cropped sleeves over wrist-length, dresses with tabards and aprons, and a rich mixture of patterns. Long hair was layered and women wore platform espadrilles laced up the legs. The clean-up came in 1976, when women adopted men's tweed jackets for day, and black tie and tux for dress-up evenings, but not until 1979 did *Vogue* finally blow the whistle on 'a decade of onion dressing'.

THIS was the decade of women's lib, when the dolly birds and chicks of the sixties decided they had had enough. The movement began in the US with the 1963 publication of Betty Friedan's *The Feminine Mystique*, which revealed to women the cathartic question 'Who am I - other than X's wife and Y's mother?'

'Man isn't the enemy, he's the fellow victim' Betty Friedan explained to *Vogue*, describing women's 'guilt about working and being successful' and 'the vacuum if you stay home'.

The key figure in the argument was Germaine Greer, opposite. Her intelligent and beautifully written book *The Female Eunuch*, published in Britain in 1970, gave rise to ten years of journalistic debate and dinner-party bickering. Her argument was that women do not suffer from penis envy as Freud taught, but from the castration and distortion of the natural female personality. *The Female Eunuch* came

out in the USA with a first printing of 75,000 copies, and serialization in three leading American magazines. It provoked swipes from Norman Mailer, whose now forgotten *Prisoner of Sex* had recently been published. Kathleen Tynan interviewed Germaine Greer for *Vogue*, and found her 'boldly dressed and bra-less ... funny, outrageously coarse and direct about her pleasures ... a born teacher'.

Ms Greer, then lecturer in English at Warwick University, underground journalist, singer, dancer and actress, argued that it was not reform we needed but a revolutionary change in our social structure. What we had to do was open up a bigger landscape, 'retrieve our power of invention', unleash our particular female energy on a world badly in need of it. 'To be *in* love is to be in dead trouble and to be deficient in the power of living and understanding the other person' she said. 'The warning signal is when you're more anxious about losing the other person than seeing that they're happy, for then you lose your power of benevolence. What I'm supporting is a tenderness in sex which doesn't involve that edge of insecurity which makes you clutch, when you're only meant to take hold.' Her aim was to get the message of women's lib across, whether it meant writing about the hazards of going to bed with Englishmen who are likely to suggest 'Let's pretend you're dead', or 'not losing your temper when people ask you for the millionth time "Do you hate men?" ' Another liberationist, Midge Mackenzie, described Germaine Greer as 'a phenomenon, a super-heroine ... who raises the possibilities for other women. Although some of them feel that there is only room for one girl who both enjoys sex and has a Ph.D.'

After all this, that the advent of the first woman Prime Minister should pass with scarcely a ripple was the least predictable event of the seventies. As political commentator Ferdinand Mount told *Vogue* readers, the chronically able Mrs Thatcher 'has achieved something which Mrs Pankhurst would scarcely have dreamed possible - that just over fifty years after all women over twenty-one gained the vote, a woman Prime Minister would be treated as nothing much out of the ordinary'.

This 'mother of two with a taste for nice china and a husband who is a company director and enjoys playing golf' was leader of the opposition when she was interviewed by *Vogue* in 1975. Heading up a *Vogue* portfolio of eighty-five distinguished women, she had nothing very memorable to say about female power, but plenty about the state of the nation.

'We have lived like the heirs of an estate that could not be depleted' she told features editor Marina Warner '... until we awoke one morning to find the bailiff at the door'.

BY the seventies, women had lived through more changes of fashion than at any other time. In the sixties fashions were 'in' or 'out': the differences were in the looks and lengths, the accelerating pace of change, and the exclusively fashionable age group. In 1970 and 1971 clothes became pure decoration - 'decoration, not labelling', *Vogue* insisted - and the decorative revival spread outward from the houses of fashion designers to theatrical and movie circles, with hand-painted murals, ceilings sprayed with words and slogans, tigerskin-sprayed cars, cut-out

tree silhouettes for the edges of rooms, pop-painted walls, toadstool chairs and flocked tea sets.

Fashion had turned into repertoire. If clothes are modes of expression, fashion had become a vocabulary. In London you could find the whole range of fashion within a stone's throw - tweedy, ethnic, Hollywood, classic, glamorous, executive, nostalgic, pretty or international. 'The real star of the fashion picture is the wearer, the real star of the issue is you' *Vogue* was to emphasize again and again over the first half of the seventies. 'Done right, fashion now is the expression of women who are free, happy, and doing what they want to be doing ... One woman lives dozens of different lives - one at home, another at work, another out in the evening, another in the country, another in the city, and at least two more for fun.' In 1971 *Vogue* made a point of breaking all the old fashion rules, finally asking 'Is bad taste a bad thing?'

It was a milestone in the history of fashion. Enjoying this new freedom, women were no longer set pieces, arranged differently for each situation. Replacing the worn-out dress roles of the past, women were pleasing themselves with the originality and variety of their appearance, seldom conforming to anyone else's idea of what elegant meant. In the Christmas 1974 issue, *Vogue* photographed Lauren Hutton, opposite, the highest paid model so far ($200,000 a year in America for personifying Charles Revson's Ultima beauty products), make-upless, gap-toothed, tousle-haired, a 'million dollar girl next door'. In a previous issue, *Vogue* showed a kitchen gardener in her beret, muffler, wrinkled wool tights, loose mohair knitted coat, and said 'The clothes aren't smart, but they're very much in fashion. They obey the first rule of dress which is that clothes must be appropriate.'

In the 1960s fashion centered on age. In the 1970s it centred on cost as the price of a silk evening dress rose from £50 in 1970 to £300 in 1979. The fashion market resolved itself between the dead cheap - the clothes in the regular More Dash Than Cash feature - and the expensive fashion investment.

Overleaf: recurring Vogue images of the seventies included Thea Porter's evening dresses in remote middle eastern places, left, and right, Sarah Moon photographs for Biba's new Kensington department store

*Moya Bowler's shoe and boot designs, 1972, opposite, and Marie Helvin bares up
for David Bailey in Zandra Rhodes satin*

INFLATION ushered in a decade of crisis and price rises against the bleak backdrop of the three day week, the miners' overtime ban, the near demise of *The Times* and *The Sunday Times* and the ITN blackout. The streets were regularly choked with uncollected rubbish. 22 May 1973, when Nixon admitted the Watergate cover-up to the Senate Select Committee, deepened the cynicism with which most people had come to regard politics as a whole.

As moon-travel lost its thrill the nation plumped for alienation or escapism: Derek Jarman, punks and future shock, or the Silver Jubilee, *Saturday Night Fever* and the best-selling nostalgia of *Diary of an Edwardian Country Lady*. Mrs Thatcher took hold as Prime Minister and the nation staggered from near-bankruptcy to strength via North Sea oil. The eighties were launched on a rare note of optimism: the pound had climbed from 1.55 against the dollar in 1976 to 2.0821 against the dollar on 1 November 1979.

As the seventies gloom deepened, the tone of *Vogue* as reflected in its features pages became serious, if not portentous. New non-*Vogue* subjects were offered up to readers. They were treated to a quick flip through contemporary British philosophy. They learnt what new techniques of brain surgery were required to cure *Dystonia musculorum deformans*, a nervous disease marked by involuntary muscular movements and postural fixations. They translated the scientific jargon of the new industry, Futurism, and to bandy words and phrases such as Catastrophe Theory, eco-spasm and possidict. They prepared themselves for the new *gestalt* and recognized the need for feedback and fresh parameters. They discovered that dolphins were learning to speak human faster than humans were learning to speak dolphin, that number-codes would shortly be replacing doorkeys, and that the computer revolution would provide them with 'thinking' washing machines, ovens and TV sets.

'But' added *Vogue*'s expert Dr Christopher Evans, 'how easily will one be able to convince management and labour that computers, by depriving men of their jobs, are in fact freeing them for something far more exciting and worth while?'

Political theorist James Bellini wrote, 'The children of our post-war years have fed on rising expectations ... but growing numbers of that new wave youth were to be left in the cold as post-war prosperity fragmented in the poverty traps and dole queues of a failing economy ... and the highest unemployment since the Depression of the 1930s. The punk rock dandies of this particular cycle of rebellion are worthy heirs to the tradition. Johnny Rotten and Sid Vicious, Rat Scabies and Captain Sensible, the Sex Pistols, the Damned, and Clash are dead centre on the road to World War Three.'

1977 gave Punks intellectual credibility through Derek Jarman, opposite, whose film *Jubilee* began with a burning pram, portrayed Buckingham Palace as a recording studio and showed a boy being suffocated inside a plastic bag. He told *Vogue* 'I think all art should be gently subversive'.

Anthropologist Ted Polhemus defined punk style as 'provocative non-verbal communication' and told *Vogue* 'Punks look revolting ... revolting against our currently accepted standards of beauty'.

If *Vogue* readers had a nodding acquaintance with the origins of life, Big Bang theory and black holes, they were word perfect on the pollution-conservation-preservation message. In fashion captions for country clothes they read: 'Are they chopping down the trees? Ring your local C.P.R.E. branch. Is the

river filthy? Ring Friends of the Earth. Plant your own trees for posterity, nurture the dandelion and the buttercup ... hang on to the butterflies and birds, the wild flowers and the free range animals.'

They were told that we throw away enough cans each year to make a pile 45,000 miles high, that new concrete covers annually an area the size of the Netherlands, and that 130 species of animal and 20,000 kinds of vegetable have become extinct.

James Cameron reminded them that 'There is no mystery, for example, about how to cure poverty, rationalize education, abolish road accidents, and eliminate the causes of war, and probably 99 per cent of people want exactly these things. The only missing factor, as every sociologist has pointed out for donkey's years, is the ability to put the collective will and the available machinery to work.' If that factor could not be reversed 'toleration of the unacceptable will be replaced by acceptance of the intolerable'.

Casting Polaroids from Jarman's Jubilee, with Jordan as Amyl Nitrate

Overleaf: fashionably ambisexual Children of the Revolution: David Bowie, left, and right, Marc Bolan of Tyrannosaurus-Rex

THEATRE and film divided equally between escapism and exploitative violence. 'Villains are heroes now' said *Vogue* in 1971. 'Communication is brief, actions summary, titles terse. The beaten up and the beaters up, the mean and the sluttish are in the sun' and 'Is mass celebration of carnage the new drug?' asked the magazine again a few years later, marking the release of the $5 million *Rollerball. Jaws* and Sissie Spacek's *Carrie* marked a new dimension in horror, and *The Exorcist* became the fifth largest grossing film of all time.

It was a dancing decade. The theme tune from John Travolta's *Saturday Night Fever* resounded through 1978, Covent Garden played host to The New York City Ballet and *Chorus Line*, winner of nine

For nostalgia there were *The Sting, The Gambler, Shampoo, The Great Waldo Pepper*, and the seventies saw the rise of the sequel movie, *Airport 1975, The Godfather Part II, The Four Musketeers, Funny Lady* and *French Connection II.*

Celluloid imitated life as Watergate was documented in *All the President's Men*, the terrorist hijack of a jet in Uganda was fictionalized in *Raid at Entebbe*, and a nuclear leak coincided with *The China Syndrome. Star Wars* space-jumped its audiences into another world - 'a long, long time ago' - but the most original film of the decade was Steven Spielberg's *Close Encounters of the Third Kind*, grossing $400 million. It was made with the cooperation of J. Allen Hynek, founder director of the

Tony Awards, filled dance classes with a new generation of hopeful soubrettes.

There was nothing to beat Liza Minnelli's lusty *Cabaret* for sheer entertainment and Twiggy, above right, tap-danced mistily through a parody, *The Boy Friend* - but the great screen beauty of the decade turned out to be a boy, Bjorn Andresen, opposite, playing with Dirk Bogard in Visconti's ravishing film of Thomas Mann's story *Death in Venice.*

Equally decadent, Ken Russell's film *Valentino* starred Rudolf Nureyev as the brilliantined twenties pin-up, above left. Nureyev proved an impatient movie actor and told friends 'You have to be a vegetable.'

Center of UFO Studies in Illinois, who saw to it that the movie fitted the apparently genuine core of reports on the Center's files.

It took a good movie to tear people away from the box. They stayed home for *The Muppets*, the irresistibly camp *I, Claudius*, and for *Fawlty Towers.* Groucho Marx and S.J. Perelman died, but John Cleese and Rowan Atkinson lived. Despite financial straits there were some of the best series ever made for the small screen: David Attenborough's *Life on Earth*, Kenneth Clark's *Civilization*, Jeremy Isaac's *The World at War* and Jonathan Miller's *The Body in Question.*

BUT it wasn't all grim. If the sixties was a decade for going out, the seventies brought a new emphasis to the pleasures of middle-class domestic life.

Dinner party food became competitive, and newly-weds discovered an interest in good design that made Terence Conran, opposite, a wealthy man. His influence was to continue over two decades; everyone knows what you mean by 'Habitat people'. Terence Conran himself admitted that you could call the Habitat style 'Packaged Good Taste', but its success could be measured in the late seventies by twenty-two Habitat stores in Britain and eighteen more about to be opened in France, where the bourgeoisie were panting for Le Style Britannique d'Habitat. 'His eye for design,' said Antonia Williams in her interview with him, 'stems from his great love for the architecture of the Industrial Revolution, the factories and railways, locks and machinery, the work of Brunel and Morris and Mackintosh ... the basement life of Victorian and Edwardian England when things were beautiful because they were functional and because they weren't simply decorated to add grandeur to them.'

Art critic William Fever uncovered a new subspecies, Weeniculture, the province of the pocket-money generation that was spending £200 million annually on such treats as Choppers, spaghetti hoops, fish fingers, Curly-Wurlies and Bay City Rollers' concerts, and encouraged *Vogue* readers to collect ephemera. Citing the Oxford University Printer and Egyptologist, the late John Johnson, whose lifework fills several thousand boxfiles and a suite of rooms in the New Bodleian, he urged *Vogue* readers that 'nothing should be rejected on the grounds that it is too commonplace, nor should any distinction be made between the artful (Quant labels) and the artless (bingo tickets).'

JOSEPH Beuys, below, the German conceptual artist and highly-collected sculptor, who died in 1986, pioneered green consciousness and won massive support from the European young and avant garde through his impassioned appeals for a democratic anarchy. When he was sacked as a professor of the Dusseldorf Academy of Art, students demonstrated all over Germany. Maintaining 'Every man is an artist' he founded a string of Free Universities throughout Europe. 'I am struggling against the whole culture of repression' he told *Vogue* in 1974. 'Self-management ... can give the world a new form arising from the interests of all the people together.'

By the seventies David Hockney's pictures were recognized as great classics of modern imagery and the painter - reflected, opposite, against his pinboard - as one of the inspired communicators of the century. At the Royal College of Art, the Bradford-born student insisted on bringing in his own life model for figure painting, because he thought the ones supplied were too ugly. He painted his own diploma and dyed his hair 'because blondes have more fun'. He painted subjects that interested him in ways that interested him - boys in the shower, Typhoo tea packets, fish and chip shops, swimming pools, California scenes - and talked about art in a way that everyone could enjoy. 'A photograph is no more real than a painting' he told *Vogue*. 'Paintings are a *bigger* way of looking at things.' In his marvellous autobiographical book published in 1976, he wrote 'the art of the past can be treated too pompously. The truth is, the art of the past is living; the art of the past that has died is not around. The very term academic ... is really about attitudes, a drying-up, and sterility. I have always had a fear of repetition.'

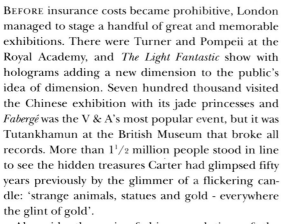

BEFORE insurance costs became prohibitive, London managed to stage a handful of great and memorable exhibitions. There were Turner and Pompeii at the Royal Academy, and *The Light Fantastic* show with holograms adding a new dimension to the public's idea of dimension. Seven hundred thousand visited the Chinese exhibition with its jade princesses and *Fabergé* was the V & A's most popular event, but it was Tutankhamun at the British Museum that broke all records. More than $1^1/_2$ million people stood in line to see the hidden treasures Carter had glimpsed fifty years previously by the glimmer of a flickering candle: 'strange animals, statues and gold - everywhere the glint of gold'.

Alongside the noisy fashion revolution of the 1960s and early 1970s came a quiet metamorphosis in the status of decorative art and clothing. The most fashionable clothes were for the first time seen in context and on a par with the other arts, even to the point of holding their value long after their day was over. By the mid seventies dealers were charging up to £100 for an antique dress in good condition, and Sotheby's and Christie's were regularly including costumes in their sales at which private collectors bid against museums.

There had been increasing signs of this since the V & A's exhibition in 1960 of Heather Firbank's clothes, 'A Lady of Fashion', but as early as 1954 Richard Buckle's Diaghilev exhibition in Edinburgh and London had displayed costumes as works of art, something over and above artefacts. A pioneer private collector, Mrs Doris Langley Moore, had opened the Museum of Costume in 1963 in the Bath Assembly Rooms, but the winter of 1971-2 was to see the most important fashion exhibition yet - Sir Cecil Beaton's 'Fashion' at the V & A, showing a collection of 350 remarkable clothes dating from the 1880s. Dazzled by Balenciagas, Poirets, Vionnets, a Fortuny and a mass of Chanels, women gasped with horror at Cecil Beaton's story of how a Chicago millionaire, whose deceased mother and wife had been famously fashionable, had made a bonfire of all their clothes, many still unopened and unworn in their Paris boxes and tissue paper, only a few weeks before Beaton had contacted him.

A number of market stalls and small shops now opened to sell dress-as-art. Magazines photographed teenage beauties wearing their ancestors' dresses - goffered Edwardian muslins and lawns, Victorian bloomers and pinafores, beaded twenties dresses, parasols and plumed hats. Some of the costumes were antiques, some fakes, but whether retro or repro the early seventies measured the high water mark of fancy dress revival, with plenty of dressing-up parties to match, and in the couture grand old traditions of embroidery and lace-work, hand-painting, drawn threadwork and pintucking gave elderly craftspeople a new lease of life.

Bernard Nevill's Renaissance prints in dresses by Thea Porter and Bellville Sassoon, opposite, worn by the Percy sisters: the Ladies Caroline, Julie and Victoria, photographed by Barry Lategan. Paper taffeta wedding dress, above left, by Bellville Sassoon, with a wealth of Edwardian detailing. Julie Christie, above right, in tunic and leggings by Fortuny, whose dresses were collected by Eleonora Duse, Sarah Bernhardt and the Marchesa Casati Stampa. Julie Christie had just added to her Fortuny collection with a pink and silver dress bought at Christie's.

*Bryan and Jerry and
John and Yoko*

A fter the excitement of the sixties, it was a phlegmatic and frequently bitter decade. As Andy Warhol put it 'In the sixties everybody got interested in everybody ... The sixties were clutter. The seventies were very empty.' It was an inconclusive period of action and reaction as the future of the future came into doubt. The divorce rate rose and men, already confused by women's lib, read with alarm of Lee Marvin's ex-mistress in California, Michelle Triola, who in 1976 took the film star to the Supreme Court and won a property settlement in return for six years' disregarded devotion. 'The splendid Miss Triola was one woman who refused to be stuck in the women's transit lounge' wrote journalist Tina Brown. 'Instead, she hijacked the plane and demanded $2 million and a parachute.'

John and Yoko, opposite, were still together after four years, two of them as a married couple. 'Shall we cool it a little?' Lennon asked *Vogue.* 'But cooling is the hardest thing of all.'

But the final word on the change in personal values came from Britt Ekland, who said of Rod Stewart in May 1975, 'I know a lot of people didn't expect our relationship to last, but we've just celebrated our two months' anniversary.'

Most of the transformations which came to Britain in the eighties resulted from the extraordinary longevity in power of a prime minister of absolute views and formidable will. The first woman to come to the premiership, Mrs Thatcher endured longer than Palmerston to survive three terms of office and become Europe's most experienced premier.

Out of Thatcherism came the end of the social consensus, trade unionism and state monopolies and the growth of independent trading enterprise and unemployment. The rise of middle management and the Eurocrat brought a consensus of middle-class attitudes and style. Britain became greyer and more aggressively business like. The new billionaires who attempted style seldom had any - the Richard Bransons and Andrew Lloyd Webbers.

Sophisticated technology made possible the information explosion, the fax machine, newspapers the size and weight of telephone directories, factory automation and increased flexibility of product design. In an opposite and inevitable reaction, the Yuppies, popularly supposed to inhabit Docklands warehouses full of chrome and glass, lined their urban nests with acres of Laura Ashley sprigged wallpapers, scrubbed pine dressers, festoon blinds and chintz-covered tables straight from a Victorian rectory. Car-ports and garages added tens of thousands of pounds to the price of living in the city.

By 1990 the British had had eleven years to get used to the unique configuration of national leadership by two grandmothers, almost identical in age, but very different in style. While the Queen continued to absorb every part of herself into her role, time completed the evolution of a prime minister whose office became an extension of her personality.

Vogue called Mrs Thatcher 'the best-pressed premier', and in 1985 she agreed to be photographed for the magazine by David Bailey and gave readers the benefit of her fashion advice, which proved to be as dogmatic as her political philosophy. 'I have bought about two suits a year' she said. '... In the last two years, the shoulders have been a little wider, the tops of the sleeves a little more important. That's the only genuflection I make to fashion.' Off the subject of clothes, she told readers that when they called her 'inflexible' what they really meant was 'firm'.

'I think, historically, the term 'Thatcherism' will be seen to be a compliment.'

her from English rose to the svelte and ravishing beauty, opposite. *Vogue*'s frequent portfolios of her public appearances and foreign tours over the eighties documented every change of hairstyle and dress, while British fashion thanked providence for providing its best-ever ambassador.

In August 1987, with pictures of Boy George in badges and Princess Diana in Rifat Ozbet, *Vogue* identified pop stars 'and the increasing fashion consciousness of the young royals' as the potent media images of the decade. 'For the New York teenager, the European or Japanese housewife' wrote *Vogue*'s Sarah Mower, 'British fashion means pop video on MTV and splashy Di and Fergie cover stories in weekly magazines. To the world at large, our style is that which is worn by youth at its class extremes: British fashion in international markets is Rock 'n' Royalty ... and they dress to be noticed.' In place of film stars, *Vogue* now photographed Madonna, Prince, Billy Idol and Michael Jackson.

The famous-for-being-famous model stars of the early nineties: from left to right, Naomi Campbell, Linda Evangelista, Tatjana Patitz, Christy Turlington and Cindy Crawford

Overleaf: Prince, 1990: 'he's unsavoury and he knows it'. Madonna, 1989: 'Like a Prayer is about the influence of Catholicism in my life'

The star of the decade was Lady Diana Spencer, whose public debut, her wedding to the Prince of Wales, was carried out before a worldwide television audience of 750 million viewers. Nineteen, youngest daughter of the Earl Spencer and the Hon. Mrs Peter Shand Kydd, Lady Diana was a fit heroine for the yuppie decade. Precisely what journalists Anne Barr and Peter York had dubbed a Sloane Ranger, she had grown up with ponies and dancing lessons, shared a flat in the Old Brompton Road, bought her Peruvian sweaters in Fulham and played a hard game of tennis. She was close to *Vogue*'s territory: her sisters even worked on the magazine. After the birth of her two sons a metamorphosis took place which transformed

Looking back over the eighties in 1990, *Vogue* recognized a decade of Trash Culture, noting that *Rocky Horror* was back, *Roseanne* topping the ratings and that film director Pedro Almodóvar and his trash goddesses had arrived in a garbage truck for the Madrid premiere of *Tie Me Up, Tie Me Down.* Talking of his penchant for mass murderers like John Wayne Gacy, John Waters explained to *Vogue* writer Barney Hoskyns 'All we're talking about is a certain sense of irony, and a love for everything you were raised to despise.' If the world now preferred Donald Trump's Taj Mahal casino to the Taj Mahal itself, *Vogue* concluded, the triumph of the superficial was complete.

WE had been promised that computer screens would eliminate most of our paperwork, but the tide of papers continued to rise and bureaucracy proliferated. All over Britain, in all kinds of jobs, the pressure was on. Commodity brokers and agribusinessmen ransacked their Filofaxes for a window to log in a 7.30 am business breakfast. Wives and husbands made diary appointments to get together for supper. Answering machines took messages from friends and lovers who never had time to meet. It took two earners to pay for the approved 'lifestyle', and with divorce or separation came the unravelling of financial security to add to the guilt and anguish of a broken home. Women took on executive jobs and single-parent families became common.

Women jogged or worked out before the office, dealt with domestic crises on the phone, and hurried home to play with the baby before tranforming themselves into sex objects for dinner out. 'I've got a head for business' boasted Melanie Griffiths in the film *Working Girl* '... and a bod for sin.'

In *The Fatigue Factor*, Deborah Hutton wrote that international surveys highlighted the fact that modern women are worn out.

'Fortunately, there are signs that women are no longer subscribing to the myth that they can do it all, but resolving instead to do less - dropping their commitments, so they can do fewer things better, leaving room for just being and enjoying, allowing home and family to come back into focus.'

Vogue's health and beauty pages regularly focussed on stress and fitness programmes turned from mystical exercises and general aerobics to specific workouts on machines in the gym.

Muscle-building for a 'forceful new womanhood'

EXPENSE account dining brought large numbers of new restaurants to city centres and suburbs, and cooking ran the gamut of fashion and nationality from nouvelle cuisine to Cajun. Hard-working professionals exhausted themselves with competitive dinner parties, and girls who had had a fortune spent on their education devoted their lives to concocting tasty lunches for directors.

Wine bars, supposed to be feminine alternatives to pubs, never quite took off. In the end pubs expanded the ploughman's lunches into a choice of hot plates and vegetarian dishes, and reformed their too-masculine atmosphere.

The New Londoners flaunted their money in Brompton Cross, where Terence Conran had launched his first Habitat in 1964. It wasn't until style-purveyor Joseph Ettedgui began opening up across the road twenty-one years later, that the foundations were laid for what would become London's most exuberant new catchment area - the yuppies' 'sexy' heartland. The Brasserie, the Porsche Centre and a popular pub were finally endorsed by the liner-sized Conran shop in the Michelin Building, magnificently restored in 1987, the year of the Big Bang, and Joseph's confident new Store opposite. Together with nine or ten notable restaurants, the Michelin Mile remains one place that does not shut up, like most of London, at 5.30 pm - and café life here is constantly enlivened by the possibility of spotting the Princess of Wales buying frocks or the Duchess of York ordering her veggies.

Food was a major preoccupation. Marks & Spencer put its muscle behind quality convenience foods in clinical packaging, specially for high income two-earner households. The intensified new agribusiness was not always in tune with the public concern about health. The spectre of lysteria and salmonella lurked behind the serried ranks of ready-made meals. Microwaves, it seemed, did not solve every problem. Basic food such as eggs and cheese became suspect. Scientists, politicians and doctors were all seen to be fallible, but it was the farmers who were most criticized. Public uncertainties surfaced in a return to the nostalgic, wholesome values of kitchen garden and home farm. Popular television programmes of the decade were the round-the-year series about the recreation of a traditional walled vegetable garden and Edwardian kitchen operated by a head gardener and a cook who had worked in similar establishments in their youth. The National Trust doubled its membership. Looking at grand houses, gardens and parks became a favourite weekend activity. A distaste for the practices of factory farms, the incidence of 'mad cow disease' and the pursuit of a high-fibre diet discouraged people from eating as much meat as they had in the seventies: the Waleses, said *Vogue* 'eschew red meat in favour of fish and vegetables'.

Tessa Traeger's clever and beautiful pictures of food decorated the pages of Vogue through the eighties

VOGUE kicked off the decade by introducing its readers to the new world of the silicon chip. 'Marshall McLuhan's global village may be here by 1990' wrote Antonia Williams. 'Then the separate pockets of amazing muddle in which man lives will be elevated into a far greater dimension. Global amazing muddle...' The chip, *Vogue* revealed, was approaching the molecular size and structure of life itself. 'It is a computer of such power that it can execute literally millions of operations a second. In basic number crunching it can perform a calculation with 5,000 variables in less than one second. A mathematician with pencil and paper could not do a seven variable calculation. He knows how but it would take more than his lifetime.'

The gaspable, ungraspable new civilization, readers learnt, would not only bring us a technological wonderland of no-key entry to our houses, computer-aided graphics, car-design, architecture and engineering, lighting triggered by motion detectors, and clothes-ordering from computerized warehouses, but also microprocessors to plot our car journeys, diagnose our illnesses and even position the twenty-three surviving pieces of a broken Etruscan pot for archaeologists at the British Museum.

By the end of the eighties houses were protected by heat-sensitive security lamps and cities shrilled with burglar alarms. Despite the terrifying rise in crime, most of them had usually been set off by mistake.

All set to rocket us into the seamless techno-logical Arcadia, Sir Clive Sinclair, the inventor/entrepreneur of the pocket calculator, pocket television, a digital watch and an electric vehicle, told *Vogue* 'The Industrial Revolution replaced men's muscle with machines; the revolution we are now beginning to see is about replacing men's minds. The first to go are those of men on the production lines.' Predicting a machine with 'at least the complexity of the human mind' within ten years, he recommended computers as teachers for children because of their 'infinite patience and great wisdom'.

The techno-revolution helped blur all the boundaries and divisions of the fashion industry. Designers now plan their collections for maximum video impact, and international fashion shows have become theatrical spectacles that only partially reflect the clothes you can buy. Fashion writers crouch over word processors instead of typewriters. Art editors lay out their pages with Desktop Publishing software. Pattern cutters work on computer instead of card, sending the instructions from the screen to numerically controlled cutters on the factory floor which slice through two hundred layers of fabric at a time. Fashion photographers such as David Bailey make television commercials for cars and chemicals, while film directors such as Ridley Scott make commercials for scent.

Fashion has become a vast international conglomerate, with high finance moving into the luxury goods market. In the couture, Yves Saint Laurent became a public company and the rue Faubourg St Honoré boasted the first new haute couturier to be established for twenty years, Christian Lacroix. The going got tougher and both long-established and new designers crashed, while AIDS thinned the ranks of talent world wide. Surviving designers started a range of less expensive lines and quivered under the strain of up to twenty collections a year. In London, in the shadow of the sensational new Lloyds building, the design interface thrived. Fashion designers made chairs and furnishing fabrics, world-famous architects designed clothes shops, and Joseph Ettedgui pioneered the selling of furniture and ceramics side by side with frocks.

Three great architects were working in Britain concurrently: Norman Foster, James Stirling and, left, Richard Rogers

'Shopkeepers and restaurateurs have become the new patrons of the younger generation of architects' wrote *Vogue*'s Liz Jobey in 1988, '... providing a public proving-ground for their talents.' The designer in question was Nigel Coates, a regular in the stylish British magazines *Blueprint* and *The Face*, who had transformed shops for Jasper Conran and Katharine Hamnett, and who described one of his schemes to *Vogue* as 'Noah's Ark meets the Parthenon during the Etruscan period with skyscrapers'.

'Design is a new word, a smart word' said the dynamic Jocelyn Stevens at his inauguration as the new Rector of the Royal College of Art, proposing to meet Sir Keith Joseph's higher education cuts by doubling the number of students at half the extra cost, and changing the face of industry.

'Industry is screaming for help and the College is screaming for commercial and industrial practice. I will make that bridge.' Four years later, after drastic changes and a chessboard scenario of staff moves, there was a certain defensive aggression in his attitude. 'The purpose of what we are doing here is actually connected up with the major needs of commerce and industry in this country. If that's philistinism then the person who wrote the charter of this place was a philistine and I'm the right philistine to do the job.'

France, meanwhile, had settled into a cool modernism heavily influenced by the twenties and thirties. Mitterand's Paris teemed with adult playground architecture, yet the heart of the city remained unspoiled in a way British cities did not. True to form, Docklands, it turned out, had been developed randomly and without a master plan. Prince Charles made his *Vision of Britain* television series and a late conservationism set in. People chained themselves to trees scheduled for felling, and public outcry saved many a building from destruction. 'We are suffering from an overdose of colour' French design guru Andree Putman told *Vogue*, and the anarchic Philippe Starck, above, designer of the Prat Fall chair, described his new Café Costes in the Place des Innocents: 'as beautiful and as melancholy as the railway station buffet in Prague'.

By the mid eighties this asceticism was universal, and black was the only fashionable colour. Women in black sweaters, tight black pants and flat black ballet slippers climbed into small black cars and drove home to minimal black and chrome apartments. They wrote with fat black pens in black files and put on black dresses to dance to black music in black clubs noted for reggae and rap.

THE seventies had left women in a sober mood, making decisions about who they really were, and the new decade opened with graphic Japanese origami shapes. 'Who wants to change their look every season?' asked women sinking with a sigh of relief into Issey Miyake, Yohji Yamamoto and Rei Kawakubo. 'Me!' they replied almost immediately. Two Japanese constants expanded into bigger futures: the inventive, international talent of Issey Miyake, and black.

It was the Tunisian Azzedine Alaïa who gave women back their bodies by making tube dresses that shrank until they were no bigger than swim-suits. From then on, dresses kept on shrinking until maximum lycra s-t-r-e-t-c-h was achieved. Karl Lagerfeld pronounced that legs were to be the whole fashion point of the eighties, and spindly black leggings soon took the place of trousers and skirts, while the hems of skirts crept up to jacket level. Alaïa and Jean-Paul Gaultier, Madonna's couturier and the new enfant terrible of Paris, led fashion on into areas of maximum exposure, cutting away everything but the structure so that dresses consisted of more exercise-tuned body than cloth. By 1990 miniskirts, false eyelashes and white lipstick turned the stretch look into a parody of the sixties. The Pucci Gucci look, brilliantly jazzy prints cut into body-hugging pyjamas, extended the double-take backwards into the fifties. Gianni Versace, the rock star's favourite Italian, brought his talent for stage design into his boutique couture.

Calvin Klein progressively simplified and relaxed the classic American wardrobe while in another neck of the woods the romantic Romeo Gigli brought a uniquely medieval look to the decade. The new Paris couture house of Christian Lacroix swept black away and introduced colour and spectacle, reinventing the couture as 'a laboratory for ideas'. But it was the dynamic Karl Lagerfeld - dictator of three separate fashion empires and the possessor of an alleged annual income of $4 million a year - who contributed the original and continuing eighties fashion theme when, casually juggling the famous components of the Chanel image, he produced the 'Unserious Suit'.

High-powered working women dressed in Armani, who gave women the power suit, or in clothes by the new star of American fashion, Donna Karan. Exploring the angst-ridden boundaries of her own working day, she came up with instant dressing to bring glamour to the seven-hour plane flight, the persecution of the deadline, and the long day's journey into the children's bedtime. Top television soap *Dallas* - clothes designed by Nolan Miller - added the toppling shoulder pads.

Once the shadowy figure behind a label, the designer was emerging to make videos and in-store appearances, star in his own advertisements and host charity galas. A fourteen-page advertising campaign for Ralph Lauren in 1981, for instance, had introduced the new Polo shop in Bond Street with a full-page picture of the billionaire Manhattan designer in his usual denims and cowboy belt. In the eighties the successful designer learned to take on a starring role. Today the press documents his social life, photographs his houses and dissects his private affairs.

Ribbon stretch by Giorgio di Sant'Angelo, opposite. Below, five-pointed silk by Issey Miyake

Jean-Paul Gaultier, taboo-breaking fashion maestro, and his 'Just two Cornetti' dress.

Saying 'In France we're paralyzed by chic' he dressed men in gingham and open-toed high-heeled sneakers, and Madonna in crucifixes and sex-shop corsetry. Towards the end of the eighties what interested the French underground most was the mixing of opposites: with video director Jean-Baptiste Mondino and graphics guru Jean-Paul Goude, Gaultier emerged as a great communicator, administering enough sexual, social and cultural shocks to rearrange the world through the medium of the young.

The Gaultier collections are, for the sexually hip and the media, the only shows in town; but he is also a superb tailor and has an annual turnover of $120 million

Visual parodies of the fifties and sixties filled the fashion pages of the eighties. Bodice, Azzedine Alaïa, leggings, Liza Bruce, opposite. Jasper Conran dress, Graham Smith hat, top left. Clothes by Jaeger, top right. Norma Kamali swimsuit, bottom left and, bottom right, clothes by Thierry Mugler

IT was Bruce Weber who provided one of the most influential contributions to fashion photography through his portfolios for *Vogue*. He would take a group of his friends and stars to a remote spot on the map and photograph them over the course of a few days spent together, producing pictures which had the intimacy and reality of a private album. In glossy catalogues photographed by some of *Vogue*'s top photographers - Weber, Peter Lindbergh, Snowdon, Patrick Demarchelier, Arthur Elgort - companies such as Ralph Lauren, Calvin Klein, Issey Miyake, Paul Smith and Comme des Garçons sought, not to sell clothes, but to project an image and a personality, just as Laura Ashley's catalogues had provided a context for her sprigged cottons and traditional wallpapers. The clothes were secondary to the portraits and often at the mercy of the casual treatment meted out to them by the models.

'There is a way of finding out if the catalogues work or not, but the answer does not come in retail figures' Yuki Meakawa, Comme des Garçons's London representative, explained to *Vogue*. 'What is important is that everybody wants one of our catalogues, people talk about them. The function that catalogues perform is fixing an image in the mind, and the image, a move away from direct selling, sells clothes.'

As the eighties drew to their finale it became clear that fashion's ready-made answers were debunked and style had become personalized. Dresses were demoted to frocks and clothes-fanatics became fashion victims. In a 1990 television programme called *Style Trial*, people were judged by their taste in music, clothes and design.

'Fashion is what you're offered' said model and actress Lauren Hutton 'And style is what you choose.'

The eighties also saw the death of an early prophet of style, Diana Vreeland, former editor-in-chief of American *Vogue* and special consultant to the Costume Institute, Metropolitan Museum of Art. Former *Vogue* colleagues fondly remembered a loopily arrogant fashion attitude, now sadly relegated to the past.

'We're going to eliminate all handbags!' she once told bemused members of staff. Or 'One thing I hold against Americans is they have no flair

for rain'. She announced herself a great believer in vulgarity '... if it's got vitality. No taste is what I'm against!' And a friend recalled a typical Diana Vreeland response to the Second World War: 'What amazing attitudes those marvellous people the English can conjure up! Especially when they are in trouble. Think of the Marquess of Bath, who owned Longleat. He went through the whole war with a duck on a lead, praying for bombs to fall so that his duck would have a pond to swim in.'

Adventures in the woods with Bruce Weber

Overleaf: Photographs by Herb Ritts, left and, right, Peter Lindbergh

'TURNED on any good books lately?' asked *Vogue* in 1980, previewing some of the decade's forth-coming television adaptations - including Malcolm Bradbury's *The History Man*, which shot to fame the febrile Anthony Sher, Nancy Mitford's *Love in a Cold Climate*, and Evelyn Waugh's *Brideshead Revisited*. The latter, appearing in an extravagantly stylish series of ninety-minute episodes, cost $4 million and was previewed several times in the magazine. A Granada epic starring Jeremy Irons, Anthony Andrews and bear, Claire Bloom, Sir Laurence Olivier, Stephane Audran and Phoebe Nicholls, it also starred Oxford, as itself, and Castle Howard as Madresfield. Its impact on magazines was even greater than that of other visually remarkable films of the decade, such as *A Room with a View*, *Out of Africa* or *Dangerous Liaisons*. Evelyn Waugh said of his great and snobby novel 'I am writing a very beautiful book, to bring tears, about very

The Common Pursuit,
produced by Brian Eastman,
starred a few of the best
comedy actors of the decade,
opposite. Clockwise from the
top, John Gordon-Sinclair,
Stephen Fry, the handsome
Rik Mayall, John Sessions,
Paul Mooney
and Sarah Berger

rich, beautiful, high-born people who live in palaces and have no troubles except what they make themselves, and those are mainly the demons sex and drink' and 'In the spring of 1944 it seemed that the ancestral seats which were our chief national artistic achievement were doomed to decay. So I piled it on rather, with passionate sincerity. Brideshead today would be open to trippers, its treasures rearranged by expert hands.'

The real lives of past aristocracy were portrayed in *Vogue* in an extract from Christopher Simon Sykes' book *Country House Camera*, a delightful collection of amateur photographs of the privileged at play.

One showed a gentleman learning to ride a bicycle in front of his country house, balanced between butler and agent.

If the dominating memory of theatre in the eighties was of Andrew Lloyd Webber's seemingly endless series of pop musicals, there was plenty of fine acting around for those who wanted it.

Actor of the decade award might have gone equally to John Hurt for his ability to sensitively portray John Merrick, the Elephant Man, from behind a seven-hour daily make-up job, or to Ben Kingsley for Richard Attenborough's *Gandhi*. For many, Kenneth Branagh's 1985 RSC *Henry V* was the memorable theatrical event of the decade. But after sparkling performances as varied as Cecil in the Merchant Ivory production of E. M. Forster's *A Room with a View*, below left, and the exuberant East-Ender in *My Beautiful Laundrette*, no one could deny Daniel Day-Lewis's right to succeed to the pantheon of the greats still performing well into the eighties. For spellbinding horror, 1991 provided a chilling movie vehicle for Anthony Hopkins and Jodie Foster in *The Silence of the Lambs*.

Vogue photographed Sir Ralph Richardson, Lord Olivier, Dame Peggy Ashcroft, Sir Alec Guinness and Sir John Gielgud for posterity - and recorded the new comic talents of the explosive Rik Mayall of *Twentieth Century Coyote* and Soho's *The Comic Strip*, and the sardonic, doomed Rowan Atkinson.

Alan Bennett's *Talking Heads* series of monologues demonstrated that comedy can be tragedy and that from time to time British television is the best in the world. Roger Rees waltzed his audiences through an epic on-stage televised *Nicholas Nickleby*, and John Wells took the prime minister's husband before the footlights in *Anyone for Denis?* at the Whitehall Theatre. Rock spectaculars became instantaneous world entertainment through global satellite linkups, and solo musicians with their backers filled stadiums the size of Wembley.

In a decade which reshuffled publishing houses like a pack of cards, the biography, carefully researched or simply scandalous, was usually the big bestseller. But it was a feminist press, Virago, which produced some of the most absorbing reading of the decade. Since its inception in 1976 the row of dark green paperbacks with charming and complementary portrait covers had become a passport to the discovery and rediscovery of marvellous women writers, many of whom had become obscure. The name to emerge from the founding of Virago, at first under the aegis of Quartet Books, was Carmen Callil, the curly-haired, deep-voiced chairperson of Virago and simultaneously publishing director and joint managing director of Chatto & Windus in 1982. She reprinted Christina Stead, Rebecca West, Stevie Smith and Rosamond Lehmann - who said, gratefully, 'Now I know that my redeemer liveth'.

In the eighties reggae filled the airways, fashion designers tacked pictures of Mike Tyson and Frank Bruno to their pinboards and the top black models - led by the gamine Naomi Campbell, with her golden eyes, Louise Brooks bob and Betty Boop skirts - right, appeared and reappeared on the fashion pages. Graphics designers on weekends to Paris sought out copies of Jungle Fever by photographer Jean-Paul Goude, style guru of Grace Jones, and black dancers and opera singers stole the leading roles

THE eighties were the decade when public awareness of human misery was raised through the consciences of pop stars. Mass charity events such as Fashion Aid, attended by Bob Geldof and a cast of thousands at the Albert Hall in November 1985, were a new way of fund-raising and contributing. *Vogue* constantly reminded its readers that we share 'Only One Earth' and prodded them in the direction of the green economy. 'One quarter of the world's people use up to two-thirds of the world's resources ... a forest the size of Wales is destroyed every month, ten million starve and their number increases by nearly a quarter of a million every day'. The caring new world message embraced tribal persecution, drought, flood, homelessness and poverty, and 1991 brought a terrible new phrase into our vocabulary: 'compassion fatigue'.

AIDS decimated the talents of the fashion industry. *Vogue*'s experts told readers that by 1995 every family will know someone living with, if not having died of, the HIV virus, and asked how we will cope. 'Until we resolve our own fears, we are unlikely to give love and support ... instead we are more likely to unload our own fears of sexuality and dying'.

Progress in post-Liberation sophisticated thinking about the nature of male and female was summed up by Jacquetta Hawkes, Mrs J. B. Priestley, in her foreword to *A Quest of Love*, printed in full by *Vogue*.

'Men and women are made up of varying proportions of masculinity and femininity. The 100 per cent male or female is usually a most objectionable person ... woman and man are poles apart, but like North and South, together forming the true axis of our single humanity. The masculine principle is already over-weighted in the modern world. If the ideas of some of the more strident champions of Women's Liberation could be implemented then this lack of balance would increase disastrously. Civilized mankind would become even more violent, authoritarian, over- intellectualized, fragmented...'

Vogue consciousness continued to expand. The way had been indicated by *Vogue*'s wildlife conservation feature of 1970 with the then editor Beatrix Miller committing the magazine to an editorial policy of excluding furs from threatened wildlife, an initiative which induced The World Wildlife Fund to advertise in the magazine, commencing with the Real People Wear Fake Fur campaign. The same thoughtfulness has continued with the present editor Elizabeth Tilberis, who says 'We stopped running fur features as such in 1987, although you may still see the odd piece of fur trimming here and there in the magazine. We share the concern, of course, but we also feel fur is just not fashionable any more. It's superfluous to a modern woman's needs and with the new quilted fabrics there are plenty of glamorous and warm alternatives.'

Virtual extinction of the fur business in this country came largely due to the hard-hitting advertising campaigns of the small and dynamic LYNX organization which commenced operations in 1985 with David Bailey's brilliant cinema commercial showing a bloodspattered fur fashion show and its accompanying poster 'It takes forty dumb animals to make a fur coat - and one to wear it'. Other advertisements asked 'How would you like your fur, madam? Gassed, strangled, trapped or electrocuted?' By 1990 London's leading stores had shut their fur departments. Anita Roddick OBE opened her first Body Shop in 1976 on a £4,000 loan and inviolable principles: no animal testing, no hype, minimal packaging, and respect for the environment. Today her company is worth £500 million.

Exposed by the media as never before to the horrors of the laboratory and factory farm, animal liberation was high on the public's list of concerns.

'Animal rightists say that our grandchildren will be as horrified by the present oppression of animals as we are by the past oppression of blacks' wrote *Vogue*'s Deborah Hutton. 'If you reply that the issues are completely different because blacks are people and animals are not, you do not diminish their argument. You lay yourself open to a new charge: speciesism ... Animal liberation looks set to be to the second half of this decade and the 1990s what gay liberation was to the 1970s and women's liberation was before that.'

Vivienne Westwood, world-famous nonconformist British fashion designer, found her inspiration in the 'untouchable' areas of city life to give us rubberwear, bondage trousers and ripped T-shirts from gay gyms. More recently, fans have been able to buy the triple-tongued sneaker, coronation crowns and jewelled cod-pieces. Deciding that the tradition of the human figure had finally lost its power, she explained 'It is an artist's job to wreak violence on a culture to give it new life ... My aim is to make the poor look rich and the rich look poor'. The only fashion designer who justifies what they do in broad cultural terms, her clothes are included in the permanent collection of the Victoria and Albert Museum, and in 1989 she was voted 'one of the six most influential designers in the world'. She remains the only one of those who is not a multi-millionaire.

Conclusion

As the new decade brings with it ever more urgent concerns, style continues to eclipse fashion. Yet, if style is personalized, how can a magazine tell readers what to wear?

'*Vogue* doesn't dictate!' says Elizabeth Tilberis. 'The reader is a very intelligent woman who is perfectly able to make up her own mind. We give pointers and show the best with clarity and energy. If you want to get people excited and improve their selectivity then you need the best photographers and editors to make the clothes appealing - to knock readers slightly off balance, make them insecure and ready to accept something new and a little frightening. You try to keep changing the reader's perception about what's seductive.'

Out there, after the burst of optimism released by the elimination of the Berlin Wall, we confront the collapse of Communism, the break-up of the USSR and the redrawing of the European map. Ecological disaster threatens, the world is largely unfed and desecrated. We are in mid-recession. Post the Gulf War, the new pole of global dissent is drawn up along the Muslim and Christian line and we face the possibility of a new era of religious wars.

Britain was at war when the first edition of British *Vogue* appeared in 1916, and has been at war again on *Vogue*'s 75th anniversary. Women then reacted by bursting into ostrich feathers, gauze wings and cobwebs of pearls. *Vogue* in this month of going to press, more visually sophisticated than it has ever been, proffers Vivienne Westwood's jewelled cod-pieces worn, not very seriously, over velvet knickers.

Off balance? A little frightening? Personal as style has become, there is a way still to go and *Vogue* continues to take you there.